MOTHER OF PEARL

Rose Flint

also by Rose Flint

Blue Horse of Morning (Seren)
Firesigns (Poetry Salzburg)
Nekyia (Stride)

MOTHER OF PEARL

Rose Flint

PS AVALON
Glastonbury, England

© Rose Flint 2008

First published in the U.K. in 2008 by PS Avalon

PS Avalon
Box 1865, Glastonbury
Somerset, BA6 8YR, U.K.
www.psavalon.com

design: Will Parfitt

front cover image based upon
a wikimedia commons image from Chris 73
freely available at http://commons.wikimedia.org/wiki/
Image:NautilusCutawayLogarithmicSpiral.jpg
under the creative commons cc-by-sa 2.5 license

back cover photo of Rose Flint by Samantha Jane Kerr

ISBN 978-0-9552786-6-2

CONTENTS

DEDICATION

***To my lovely and
very much loved daughters,
Lily and Holly***

"Remember you are all people
and all people are you.
Remember you are this universe
and this universe is you."
– Joy Harjo '*Remember*'

MAKING SOMETHING STILL

On each train journey this winter I watch for the deer
to step from forest shadows into delicate light
where Christmas geese are folded on green ochre; there
the river runs black, cold as cut ice, perfect mirror.

If I let go the city handrail, open my throat like a thrush,
if I place leaves and moss inside my boots,
if I go to the official station and hand over my cards,
my phone, my keys and earrings, if I trust the route

I could still make something of this last light.
I would have to move silently between the white geese
sleeping heaped like white amaryllis, step slight
and empty over the icy bitten grass to enter

the clear early air, where the wary doe waits
to watch me close my eyes. Then I would be living
the lit green fuse, the wave and the particle, the poem,
the place where everything connects: the beginning.

NOW VOYAGER

I have seen a boat swim into the earth
floating through the tide race of green weather
letting go gracefully, unlacing into grass
each slow season another fathom down.

Timbers splintered by the quick wake
of may's milky spray, her hull has thinned
to the finesse of silk, grey as winter water;
her compass facing west, is seized by stone.

There is no mast raised now
no tree of dreams that swing to catch the wind
sheets of naked white that praise the sunlight
take the writing of each storm, each dawn.

She is no ocean-rover lading stores of amber;
she holds herself broken, open
her ribs are spars that lattice only light
her only freight a wren's egg laid on lichen.

Exchanging halls of salt for palaces of amethyst
she discovers in herself the roots of oak trees
and in the dark endless voyage beneath her keel
a crystal wheel of uncharted stars for solace.

SELKIE ON LLEYN

At the sea's rim, pink thrift like twists of organdie
are stowed in crevices of rock, frail breaths
on slately rain-faced stones
that mark the island's tessellated edge.

Five fathoms down the seal has made her own territory,
returns each year to come up close
to Spring seasons like this: small flowers,
a mizzle rain that mists the distant gorse
to blurred fire and beads the turf with melted glass.

In sun, the seal's dim pool will clear to turquoise
and she'll glide within her salted towers
wearing siren leopardskin, green to match her eyes;
now her eyes are thoughtful, huge and black as emptiness.
The water roils around her turns, dark weaves
blue and shadow, make her hidden, liquid, near.

We watch each other. I am mirrored, fractured
falling from the sky to dive headlong beside her
as all around me, streams of silver air
pull tighter, slide along my skin a seal's kiss:
the world is water, cold and alien on my lips.
In all this space, only the seal's eyes are human, promising.

As I turn away the glass betrays me and I
slip, slide towards her and the waves
until my fingers catch on flowers, latch into the rock

then she swims towards me, makes me choose.

ABOVE SAINT CYBI'S WELL

Saint Cybi's ravens are seeing-off marauding herring-gulls
in a black/white war inside the wind above
the towering beech trees. I'd always cast the seagulls
as the bad guys, its those hooked-back pre-historic wings
like flick-knives and how they've threatened me
in seaside alleys where the deli's leaving spilt an easy crust.

And seagulls have no wisdom myths attached like leashes
to their legs, connecting threads that tie us
bird to human heart. Seagulls are always bird and alien,
but Raven speaks our many-storied tongue: their druid voice
prophesise approaching death and rain that brings resurgence,
Raven is our helpful spirit-guide, our guardian and healer
and Raven is the Morrigan's vicious wartime pet
that feasts on dying sight. Ravens are one-eyed Odin's seers,
Memory and Thought and Raven is the Trickster.
Only anonymous long-drowned sailors are shut inside
a seagull's head; you can see them glare out resentfully
through those sea-cold yellow eyes, always fathoms under.

Raucous, elegant, the ravens float and wheel,
returning to their roost. There's good pickings for them here,
I count a dozen sheep skulls whiter than the loaves of quartz
that build the lowest walls of ancient huts half-lost
beneath the gorse. Enough to feed a family
nine times over nine. Here, in this high place, wind starves
against stone and the silver-sheeted sea
is hammered over distance by the cold, to lie as still as death
or enchantment, and as devious. Oh love, who told you
it was better to stumble blindly up the mountain
to die alone, than to stay and fight
for another hour in the raw beauty of the air?

Sometimes it seems that nothing has a plan.
Its all tumbled anyhow, like this mossy rockfall,
like those dead brown leaves rolled inside the heart's cave
of a stripped-out ewe's carcass, like the moody sea.
I can't answer any of the questions. I can only watch patterns
forming in the air as the great black birds soar and swoop
the edge of life searching out the little hunted deaths,
the failures of breath or mothering. If I stay here longer
miracles of warm sun and basking snakes might happen
or I could freeze forever into the wheezy hollow
of my hurting chest where my energy is turning into dust.
Either way, there will still be ravens here, nesting in tall trees,
shadow wingspans circled on the wind. Yesterday I did not see the
way their presence altered light. Nor what would heal me.

GALLT Y WIDDAN

Hill of the Witch

Has she gone into the wary heron
that pleats her great feather cloak
into stillness and stands
wings of slate and her stone headstalk
carefully pivoting, all the awareness
of river's jade, river's citrine,
river's dark quartz
in her black avid eye, kindled blade beak?

Or has she fled gently into the blue smoke
of the bells or the bride-white blackthorn?
(Needlethorns longer than thin fingers,
sharp, dangerous to the heart.)
Is she here in the guise of a fly?
Does she lie in the snake's tight bed
of bracken, or the blue egg
or the spotted snake's head fritillary?
Has she shifted
into the young black bull stamping the juices
from crushed green garlic and wild violets?
Is she crouched in sorrel's white star?

She is here,
speaking under the river's raucous voice:
Listen to me, listen, listen to me...
She is stone, she is water, she is wren,
she is the wind and her breath lifts my hair
as her presence slides over my skin.

WHITE HORSES ON LLEYN

They are drawing nearer, bringing storm;
where they are is green and spacious
a lawn beneath horizon's metalled edge
but they are beating thunder into water
racing in the weather.

Their eyes are silver, their jade hooves
make a thousand moon-signs
a river laid on light;
the sea is falling from their speed
in broken necklaces of peridot,
their white hides sweat with pearl
but their muscles trawl the deep
like molten steel hawsers
pull the engine of their leap above
the highest matchstick mast
or tide's last marker on the arc of land.

On the moor, a herd of small grey ponies
raise their salted faces, gaze towards the waves.
They wheel together, restless bodies
plunging under gorse, seaspray
lifting manes to seagull feathers
as they catch the tide's new weather and
break – take flight – harness speed
to streak across green turf blazing
whiteness plumed into the wind
racing rain towards the west.
And passing, leave us tracks of liquid silver
signing Time's horizons turning round the earth.

CELL AND POLLEN

At the low point there is a deeper level
and a darkness that refuses love

in this cell you are petrified
understanding fragments of bone in stone

how stratas build upon the smallest deaths
how years and earth weigh heavy

When you have been there alone long enough
when you can yield – there will be movement

an arc slight as one atom touching another
igniting a spark difficult to see in blindness

Perceive it as colour of dark: midnight patinas
of bronzed richness under the skin of coal

or remembered marine blue that you hold tight
even when the colours form crackled patterns

torn holes where the fierce entering sea
could wash away your limbs and heart

Work your fingers into the edges as if you scraped
at the mortar between bricks: space will expand

flicker old like art-films or fireworks or how it was
the day your daughter left home and your sleep burned

You don't need to do anything quickly or in a certain
right way that someone will chart. Only begin to open

and the great white cloud horses that raced across
your childhood will gather you up into summer

so you are out in the reeds of the dragonfly meadows
with rising pollen so sweet you are starting to weep.

HORSES IN THE SUMMERLANDS

Horses like snow volcanoes, ruled by love.
Horses like bronze bells, rung by love.
Coloured horses, thick-ankled,
mapping a possible landscape, a continent
called faraway-from-here. Horses like dun birds,
like red burs, like firedragons whooshing up
and over fences, my thought, my heart.
Horses with long wide warm white necks
curved round so their nostrils were close, their breath
(grass sweet) beside my hair and my hot eyes;
their sweat's sweetness, the horse-sweetness
of hay and dung and the long fields of the summerlands.
Horses who leaped and leaped over the high boundaries
that held all the hurts together in one sharp mass,
leaped like legends with wings and I went with them, leaping
and racing and sliding in the marsh-field at the forest edge
and just for a moment I had slipped out of the grip
of the dead mother and maths and my father's eyes –
because I couldn't do maths even if I could fly
and just for a moment receive the blessing
of breath so laden with sweetness it was
as if a hand stroked my hair.

HALF DEER HOUND

Summer closes over the island in the valley
even though the path remains, an old raised bank
between stands of kingcups, alders thin as pencils
and the stone signs of the mill: mossed broken walls,
the stream a sudden dressy waterfalling over steps,
an arched bridge gnarled in with roots of hazel.

Oak trees hum with flies that flick vibration
through the yellow light and darkness of the wood.
I saw two fawns here on Midsummer's Eve,
small as hares and freckled into fern and briar.
Stilled, shivering in terror, until I came too close,
then they leaped and ran, blind in desperation.
Later, I heard a deer's low bark and thought
She's called them home –

I knew their danger.
My blonde lurcher, sweet tempered hunter,
was at my side, young yet and crazy for the chase.
Killing was something automatic, yet strange to her.
The first deer she brought down – full sized –
made her howl in terror, yelp and rush enough
to send green rainbirds swooping out alarms.

Water and stone, water, stone and tree,
loamy silts of last year's leaves, black marsh ooze,
fox paths – I taste the bitter darks
of earth that bind me, guide me.
When I step beyond this place,
the deer will melt out of the bracken, the grass
rephrase itself along my tracks, rainbirds
sing their territory. They will miss me
no more than any other summer shadow, passing.

MIDSUMMER CRONES

for Ann

Up on the hill the sky widens
and we breathe for the first time today.
It's cooler as the sun settles
but we're fiery from the walk
and we shrug our jackets from our shoulders
– mine an old grey denim, once my daughter's,
her's a sweatshirt, once her son's.

The crows are finally silent. A few still
sail across the violet evening,   black mourners
                                rowing west.

My young dog is bleeding, celebrating solstice
with her first scarlet hour.
We grandmother her, stroke and fuss, remember
our first time, near enough forty years ago
and still fresh within us   that strange moon.

                Different now my blood,
a rare dry letting, full of earth signs.

Black crows, red blood, silver hair.
Summer heat beats in the grass, vibrates
each rock and flower as night
comes stately into the valley
on blackwinged, shadowed feet.
                                Time for home.
 We pull our familiar jackets closer
for warmth.   Begin the slow descent.

ROWAN AND RED THREAD

for Nina

If you think back into your emergence
from your Mother's womb you will feel the miracle
in the centre of your body as if you held within you
a chalice filled with fire. Your daughter flamed out
on the red life thread, as you had done,
as your Mother did, and beyond her all the mothers
in the clan – *some clear and close and others gone
into the mists* – reaching back into the land,
passing on this fine red cord that binds you,
turns you inside out.

And what you made between you down these years
of generation, passing on the gifts – *strength,
red hair, love of cats, second sight,
and this need for making art* – is a chain,
each link as intricate as Celtic knotwork
or the stepping reel of a Scottish dance
that winds a round about the circle
of the inner space, the centre, where you hold.

Red cord of life: *mother, daughter, mother.*
Red thread wound between the circle stones,
the streams and rowan trees of the birthing land;
your bloodline winding back and going on
beyond the distance, beyond the patterned dance.

MOTHER OF PEARL

She is skimming over the ocean towards you in a blue boat.
The sky is that intense blue of bluebells in the oakwoods
back home and the furthest sea is true indigo.
Her boat – dark blue with a white sail –
is a slight geometry laced with white foam.

There are five cranes following the wake's turquoise
curve and race. She says they will teach you to dance.
One is most ancient and has many times been a man –
No, not a fisherman, she tells me and laughs at my naivety;
lately he was a priest in an eastern country of waterfalls
and cloud-forest. No doubt this will be part of it.
In her entourage there is also a woman who is heteromorphic
and nightly may become a puma bodied like a wheatfield
in the wind or like a sunning lizard, or the sequinned
hummingbird that pierces orchids for their honey. All
is relationship; each of her different nightselves is specific.
Unhurriedly, you will learn sensuality through these creatures;
all the sevenfold wild senses, the wisdom of five elements.

Out of the sea's blue spaciousness she comes like a homing bird
to find you however far inland you go, for she is steely
and determined. All your life she has searched for your teachers
collecting them like necessary provisions, or treasures
from the bazaar. The teachers themselves are freighted
with the opulence of a thousand and one images:
a lammergeier flying high above the icy slope
of White Mountain, taking the sky in his wings like a star;
or a silent stone courtyard shimmering with heat, where
a black-veiled woman waits beneath two pomegranate trees.
Some visions will tear the fabric that you thought was you apart
and these you will not want to see but must – there is a video

of a field where war has broken up humanity; child and heart
comparable in texture to the murdered land's dust.

These are badges of faith and she is bringing the box
for you to keep them in. I have seen this: it is tiny,
mother-of-pearl, intricately carved for your tongue to caress,
your throat to swallow with ease. She will give you dark wine
and then slowly kiss your mouth, the grace of her breath
entering you fully. I know this. I have tasted her salt and sweet
and that which is bitter beyond belief, beyond desire, beyond
hope – but this is the nature of the work. This is how it begins.

CHILD OF THE SNAKE

Out at the far white edge of the harbour
I worked in a bar, that season,
lived in a rickety loft through hot months
that blistered the shutters
and a breeze that burnt off the sea.

Mornings, coffee curled on wind that I soon got to know
as brown, warm as a cat round my ankles
or full black roller pounding all thoughts from my head.
Nights out the back, Wind would stroke me like a lover
and drive me as crazy, harping on and on.
Nothing secret from his paws,
in and out of the ramshackle house
his sighs and roars startling my eyes with something
salt as memory, or good remembered dreams.

I had a baby then, that blue air summer.
Couldn't work out how the wind felt about her,
sometimes so dear and gentle rocking the cradle
I could hear it creaking to and fro
as I shone the crocks and kettles far below.
Once I found the cot fallen:
she was hanging, suspended, swinging, still asleep,
darkness
not yet descended the steep tower of her stair.

Night after night and too many shifts
and too many strangers
who watch me with curious eyes as I dip and rise,
smart evasive twist of my hips at each table,
hands scorched full of brimming dishes
– *sour cream, green chilli, catfish* –

Wind scooping the smoky scents from the porch
to the quay, moodily squalling the sea
so boats toss, uneasily shiver.
Wind, my animal partner, rolling tin suns to my feet,
amusing my daughter.
Wind my enemy, who tipped her out into space.
Devil-Wind, Santa Ana,
I feel your black fingers squeezing my mind.

At the hinge of the year weather grew sulky,
blew tides of red leaves, seaweeds and whispers of thunder
through the shaky blinds of my room.
I was moving on.
I placed the last sauce of lemongrass dead in the centre,
set the last ice in the flickering glass.
In the car I checked my inventory:
shell of the starfish, cut corn stalks, gull feather:
cold sweat pricking
something missing, forgotten –
Driver, I have left her –

Wind rushes past tearing my hair
as the car hurtles faster and faster
and we fly the wild black stair of the mountain.
Driver smiles through the mirror
as we fall down the space of the steep road
 to the deep-centred place, the wasteland
where lost children creep in the dust.
 She is there, sleeping, curled on the arid ground
and encircled by Snake
who watches with clear silvered eyes;
his clean coils are a lapping spiral.
Kyklon, Kyklon – I call him softly,
shawl my arms round her so close
that my body dissolves

and each part flows into the sound
of the single small feather beating
of her heart.

Wind comes to me then, hums sweet honey-breath
that alters old dirty air into light or lucent water,
a pool where buds unfold into jasmine blooms
and birds of paradise form and hover.
Spreading beyond us, wind ripples through greenwheat.
How delicately, how delicately, it sings.

MOONTRADE

for Lily

Lily left in a flooding month but only once I saw the Moon
and she was caught in the fur of the midnight city
like a white ghost bur twitched from a dream's seagrasses.
Then nothing. Only the nightly count, the empty cup.

Days or weeks I was on the road, on the hill, on my way
till I came round a corner and she'd come clear, risen up
full from the valley to rest on a woolsack of clouds
where she watched the city's scurrying bullion; guinea brass
to her silver coin. And this Moon is questioning me:

how am I spending my time? I'm going too fast, forgetting

tonight, in one of the hours of her long lidded night
she'll look through the window of my daughter Lily
in Mexico City, pour her silvers over her sleeping,
soothe the cicadas, the clicking Spanish guitars.

Later rain will muffle Moon under his coat and bundle her
into the deep cave of the mind where she'll lie unseen
and subversive. So far she's always escaped, in time.
Next month I'll keep better watch. Ask her to come
lit in a white flame dress
that spills love to the world's four corners.

I'll call her out with a cry/poem/prayer: *Moon, Moon*
this misty city can't make anything out of your night currency
but I'll do a trade with you. I'll set my cup in the window
of every month and sing you into its circle
if you will gift my daughter with a good dream
as she lies sleeping in the City of Magic Possibilities.

BLOOD MOON

for Holly, London 7/7/2005

O let the city hold
let the city hold her   (my daughter Holly, with green eyes,
all your daughters)
          the nearlyfull moon will rise at nine
to watch the happenings here   (even heart
hidden under hands, as if cupping a match, spark
heart as tinder)   let Moon's bloodied eye be sweet
not angry, pulling the magnets awry, letting free crackles and flash,
she must have seen my daughter walking love.

Your daughter too – going out on the town,
          to the cafés and galleries, rosé by the silver water,
     summer's taste a new place, eastern
          Turkish, Arabic, suddenly shuttered –
Walking love. Learning the street-grid, time and chance
occurring on crosses, kestrel swung above signs of money, blues
sung under the escalator, all pushed in together:
high heel sandalfall dance from the fractured kerb – look up!
stars framed by soaring columns of rooms, dark and light –
inside here there are quarrels and losses, sleepers on shift work,
                    someone learning to drum.
All our daughters, this hot night when the elder trees
on the wasteland   weep fistfuls of hard green rain into the wind
     that lifts the stink of garbage   so sour and beautiful
          and at midnight in Little Venice
white buddleia pours her arms over mossed walls
like a perfumed ghost –   like a ghost-girl
   slipping out of the smoke leaking out of the underworld
                    trying to find the way home.

Holly walks love, finding the knowledge.
She could world-walk here, and did: Spain and China, India,
child of Africa, the city's luminous spars
        arms to hold her   hold all the daughters
learning each other   ordinary always (magazines, chapbook
and chatroom, tract and text)   a miracle, new thing
on the tongue, in the hands henna and pearled nails,
in heart-and-mind, Brick Lane or the serpent river, kings and friars
and angels all pushed together in the rumbling halls of Dis
where sitting beside her is one wrapped woman shaking
finger-tracing and whispering words from her opened Qur'an
knapsack at trembling feet as they all rush towards exit
into this blood-moon pooled in the streets and the unsafe air
still   she remembers: walks love.

       Broken swollen flowing holding
           our daughters, in the dark/light rooms of their city,
in stillness, the same dream: you just walk it, walk, love.
What else is there?
The moon rising higher now
white light over rooftops the attention of heaven.
                  Someone learning to drum.

WOMEN AND CHILDREN AT THE WELL

for Sally

One woman has arranged feathers in wave after wave
of small red birds descending her back,
placing tunes in her earrings. She hens a troop
of wind-babes, chicks as free as swansdown in the sun.

One mother has a pierced child pale as a moonslice
who engages the water like newness, her hands an hourglass:
Time stops the heart. Some of us fall into attitudes of prayer:
what we grieve is the fearsomeness of love.
Two girls are black lilies, tall wands, coronas on fire;
cold fear again: at how carelessly a hand could span
their flawless bellies; their skin is licked toffee, sweet maple.
How does their mother survive each day of danger and beauty?

A small girl circles the pool's shimmer, singsonging
her incessant foreign tongue. She knows her hands already,
presses her cold palm's kiss on our bodies: three chakras,
heart, throat, forehead. Her benediction is silver grace.

Below the brightness of the water's piccolo
below soprano chants and jubilation we listen
to the voice that wails and keens her daughter's loss, her song
broken rough as iron; black as molten tar, the tang of it.

So many of us recognise the sorrow cried by that ancestral voice:
all those ruby children running past us fast as melting snow
and we sing that our daughters live: here, now, in this moment
in the spark of each drop of water a girl flings into the sun.

MOONCHILD

As she was born the silence began its long roaring.
The sand-timer shocked from a hand and absence
streaming out, stopping up eyes, mouth, ears
with its grains of seconds, flowing minutes.
They called her and called with their clever hands
but she would not come, nor could not, but came too late
silence still shut inside her, and whatever else
locked its fist on her baby breath.

I called *Let me* – held her. Time:
one grain of sand's shift and trickle against another.

Delicate grace of pearl, sea-blue print bruising
beneath her eyes and taut starfish hands shivering –
as if this unfriendly air could still become
her safe ocean: if she could hold.

Out of my window I watch an elliptic moon sail past
so fast – and tethered to her, keeping pace, a star.
Their balance touches me, their indivisibility: Atropos
cannot cut the cord between this mother and her child.

In black glass I lay undreaming, and she in white,
protected and alone; almost sleeping,
until her fingers were sifting fine shelled sand
stinging my eyes in the island wind and her feet
were dancing impossible baby tracks across the beach.

Her elusive breath slipped through my fingers
as easily as Time. At night, I thread the spindled silks
of stars between my hands, determine the matrix
of a new constellation: a small cat's cradle,
ebb and flow of light and shadow
holding her safe in the moon's crescent arms.

FRAIL BIRDS

And there are the babies who come
like frail birds
flown through a storm
to the care of this quiet room

some will fly away,
make the journey to the west
some will choose to stay
all are blessed

Each one folded close in a nest
safe under glass
each tiny heart rests
at the tip of the wave's white crest

Machines keep watch like angels
guard each dream with bells
a mother sings *Come home*
come home my little bird
her tears fall like rain
small fingers clinging
life taking breath on the wing

some will fly away,
make the journey to the west
some will choose to stay
all are blessed

FOR BRIGE AT IMBOLC

Suddenly last week I saw snowdrops
pushing through a swell of green frost

and below them a green rivered field
   was tipped with a wash of wave-energy
     shaking the grass and
         a single snowy floating swan.

And that day, in my poetry class
   a green-eyed girl with a river of long black hair
   told me she'd chose the scent
     of Mother's milk to lure a boy
       to lull him.

When love sweeps over me in suddenness
   my breasts prickle with memories
     of letting down the milk
      for all my winter babies

   the world fallen still and small
        as a snowflake

my flooded body white belled petal, green veined.

     And always the Swan, white as heaven
    flying into the days
     and this river of years
of flood and frost and green heart-fire.

WITHIN THE SPIDER WEB THE WORD

Runes written by lichen on grey rock
the heron reads and rests his angling head;
this is the time of new messages and signals,
clean dawn slants light and underlines
with shadow   River speaks
                sharp-tongue silver
and oaks finger leaves
                over and over into light;

what is spoken here –   now –
by blue fish, birds of airy graces,
              by stems, stalks,
      writing the white morning –
what is understood in the blood,
in the pulse and the spirit
      under fur or feather   or leaf or skin,
by the Green Man in his pelt of vines
by Gaia garbed as a spotted deer and dancing,
   what is sung on the wind,
                        called across earth
            fired in the berries brightness,
                deciphered by water –

are the webbing words of Spider:

            yesterday, now, tomorrow, beginning.

VIXEN

I could put my hands over my ears
but the sound is too white   blurred high-frequency,
            howling
and is inside me anyway   so what
        could I keep out?   As if the breath of a vixen
had filtered into my room's black night air
when I was sleeping
            so I am tuned now
        to cunning, doubling back, sleight of hand, light
and edge of shadow   this running fox
    with her masks and seven selves –
            that's how she hunts her freedom,
the hot guise of fur's dark stole over bare shoulders
        dancing stilettos. And I have four puppety-limbs
        and a puppety-heart jiggling in space
because fox isn't there, not there in the real.
    in the grief-place   she's out thieving
        testing the cut-throat sing of the wires
    one more time. She will only enter
the black hole inside her *in extremis* of love. Loving her children
licking their baby roly-poly arms, one side a delicate fur
biscuit-cindered by sun, the other as sweet and white
as bread; softness so deep she kisses, she nuzzles
and rolls in it, rubs her face in its bliss. Then she must
            race to the stream, river, lake or wherever
                will take the terrible stink of love away
so no one will know, ever
where to find the cave of her heart   that holds them
always safe.   So she goes
threading her way back nervously between thistles
    and thorntrees and ice, a red line of blood
        tailing out of her
anyway   the hounds already here.

GIVING FEAR TO RABBIT

So Eagle, cruising dreamily heard the cry
of Rabbit's terror
    caught it
        delicious as a lick of blood on empty air
and wondered
that the lichened stones below him
could speak of fear so eloquently.
    So he spied more, spied more, spied
a single silver whisker shivering
  O let not Eagle come, called Rabbit. *Eagle, Eagle
    do not come...*
           So Eagle came.

Give your fear to Rabbit, you said.
And for this rabbit of gorgeous black fur
straying into my garden like a sacrifice
I have spread a generous give-away feast:

Pouch-Face, taste my leafy panic of a starving future,
chew this tender terror of the loss of love,
(it's a sweet stalk and your teeth will like it,
will mark it, you will swallow it slowly as cream).
Velvet-Bag, suck on raw honey vertigo, drink deep
of this blue-clover dread of lows in the winter season.
Little Twitch-Nose, I offer you calabrese and pippin,
nibble these delicate tastes of despair
for the green wheel of regeneration: I am afraid
of the arid spirit gobbling light from the grass.
O Luck-Foot, Star-Scut, accept these tender portions,
neat juicy slices of harm and hurt to the children,
relish, absorb, enjoy.
  Rabbit eats, hops, scatters her pellets – all she has made
of my huge fears, a few round brown pellets –

she scatters them into the garden and I am so light
  I move into the wind
              light as a feather –

Silent Rabbit's pellets sink down quick and rich as rain
as new plants seed and root, leaf out in glory
under the long slow shadow of the Eagle's wing.

SPIRIT PATHS

And what I hope for every winter is to find a way through
to the other side where the jubilant light begins again
in a hesitation of birdsong.

I am learning to see in the dark, recognise that this is a sign
 and this, these sudden sensual chances and clues
– as in melodic fifths on the radio or a rain-diadem,
or the unexpected arrival of white cyclamen in cellophane –
things the body perceives first as elements of light
and offers up to the spirit, so shut in its hole, mole-blind.

And there are the synchronicities that puzzle you
but make me shiver with their meanings: three aligned
heron feathers or the time and thought of meteorites;
I bring them back to you like trophies from a race of joy.

I had always believed I would die young
not making the markers of thirty nor forty-five.
In a way then, this is all extra and more risky than any year,
this precious time of coming-to-knowing,
but even my acceptance of what is, is, can't fully protect me;
Autumn still brings the familiar fear: Winter will be here
and I will be in darkness, groping forward nervously
trying to remember that the black dragons
and dogs of shadowland are guided by dark mothers
carrying secret gifts of pearl – still I'll cry for kinder weather.

This then, is the origin of fear: that the sun will not rise
and there will be no release from the dark; this, set beside
our knowing of how we must wait always for the hour
when we will not go on into the next season.
Like a film of ghosts, the family, the quick rivers and flowers,
the music and horses will stream past us

covering the brightening land as we are turned aside
into a strangeness we can only trust.

This morning the air reminded me of the country
where we learned to love each other; I know now
that was not better than this. All our symbols and armoury
all our footsteps and collisions are spirit paths, showing
the way through, complex and simple as the lines
held by my hands; and how I hold love between them.

VAST PETALLED FACES BROAD AS SUNS

I hate the way I cannot remember names. I'm thinking of those stone caskets for the dead that I saw in Crete. I'm thinking about them because I'm drawing flowers and leaves in this margin and I often find I'm drawing these huge delicate lilies and flat leaves and reeds and deer like those that were painted on the sides of the caskets. Little magic images of life. There seemed to be some kind of emanation from the flowers – maybe perfume – but it looked more like light or a description of energy drawn in radiant lines and dots, black, red, yellow ochre.

A type of sarcophagus, Minoan. A stone box, lidded, splay-legged, small enough for only a meagre huddle of bones and dust. They bent the bodies into curled foetal form when they were still warm; shut the lid, let them go into time and dark. The museum would not allow photography so I crouched down on the cold smooth floor and drew all over my notebook. The dim light hummed with electricity. I was breathless. Curious

the attendants came to look, laughing and commenting in unknowable Greek. I was scrawling so fast! Big clumsy sketches of thin stags with long extending necks, tough young bulls that held up receptive faces to possible roses or oleanders, mythic dancing beasts with horns and horses tails. All the creatures were tiny, with dainty hooves and exaggerated noses, with big kohl-rimmed eyes. But the flowers! Tall as trees, vast petalled faces broad as suns, bending down to the animals with their rays pulsing out like gifts; and a kind of listening or sensing.

I'm growing old. I hate not remembering names. I keep thinking of calyx. It was something like that, calyx. That's a holding kind of word: Calyx. Greek. a bud case; sepals collectively forming the protective layer of a flower in bud. It's just the sound that is similar, the same shape of breath in my mouth. Now I am comforted by rhyme that soothes over loss: they were caskets for the dead and what was so miraculous was the joyous life in them.

THE KEEPER OF RITUALS

The Keeper of Rituals
spoke of the body full of snakes:
That's how you dance, she said.   Feel it!
She swayed, heavy and devious, big black cobra
disturbing our cool grey English air;
Africa in our senses.

The poor of my people still leave grave goods
for their beloved dead, she told us.
We dance their souls away, give them time
to pass through, nine days to reach their land.
Later we call their spirits back, let them live,
feed them with cornmeal or maize.
Three days we let it lie, until only
its outer seeming still remains.
Somewhere else, its vibrant energy.

We called the Ancestors in,
learned of ragged stick and washed stone,
cried out names of those we'd loved –

Later, I think of those poor New Orleans graves,
the gifts of special foods, patched coats or candles;
of how the Beaker people left small cups, and Celts
drew red ochre right across the bone.
And of Tutankhamun, Howard Carter entering there:
Well, can you see anything?
Yes, wonderful things!

Amongst the canopic chests, unguent jars
and ebony leopards –   the unseen spirit
dancing; rhythms tapping out the coded journey
of the Afterlife.

Messages for the dead, the living,
and for the unborn Ancestors, listening
in the shadows, even in the spaces between
the golden links of the Necklace of the Rising Sun,
where Heh, the god of Millions of Years
holds above his head the hieroglyph for eternity.

MORIBHAN

The air here has a white quality, is hopelessly forties, out of season.
　　The quality of the wave is white, undulant, lyrical,
　　someone placing their two hands together with one palm
　　　　　　　　　　beneath the other – like two
　　　leaping fish –　　then jiggling their arms in a wave-shape,
　　playful　　　dated as dance music.

Small houses cater for tourists in blue, white again.
　　　　　　Feathered palms extend their necks, watch all ways,
　　　　shiver　　　　with morning's apprehension of north.
　There's a latent fierceness in September;　fire is out of the sky,
　wind out of the water: something is left, abandoned
trieste　　　last night's rain is a sequinned dress
　　　　　　　　wet chiffon thrown over the benches.

　　　　　　Out on the noon sands naked men, brown and old
swim alone in the splendour of light.　　　All is cool enough.
Chairs on tables, shuttered eyes.　　The vans arrive.
　Racks of fine linens fade like flags as summer dismantles itself
breaks into tiny pieces of sun　　smearing galettes with honey
　　making the last cider cup glow　　　a dish of goldleaf.

Around the town, granite has made a different arrangement
with time　　　　deeper than this froth of seafoam seasons.
　Granite acknowledges the stars
　gives back dark　　mica　crystal　calcite　sparks.
Within this passage grave, each cut stone　　fine-grained as sky
is pocked with pattern, the surface dints and runnels
underneath my touch　　unfathomable　　so
　　my fingers slip　　inside a depths
of dark matter　　fumble the invisible, enduring universe.

When you walk out to the sun and leave me,
your receding light   creates a stone of solid shadow that falls
        to block the entrance   so I am locked alone in blackness,
shut inside the stones   so close

I hear their breathing. Now my blinded hands trace drawings:
ideas clear as maps of water, air, or love.

Granite holds some understanding of the mystery:
                such weight, density, sheer size
of death   against the frailty of a life-line drawn by leaping deer:
the Goddess here, is abstract, carved by space and rock
                into a form of solace.

Returning to the sands, I see that in my absence
the world has been made new.   Each tree   each lyric wave
hangs vivid   re-born in this moment of the autumn-tilting sky
the quiet shore   my gaze.   Sun slants in
through serpent corridors,   smoothes the walls
                sets free the shadows
so nothing stays   in stillness in these stones
    that dance like the distant sea in radiance.   For a moment
    I see you held   motionless in their dark arms
until blue waves   white sky   green grass and swaying reeds
curve around you, open out –   The town still
        sings with early evening.   There's time yet

SECRET FIRE

Mother said
that she had seen an owl-headed woman
standing by her sleep.
In her voice I felt the feathers,
their soft mottle, and something dangerous
that clung to her like dark.

We'd caught a limb-struck tawny
from the hedge, gold feathers spilt upon the road,
a track of burnished arrows
in the sun. Strange, this bird of night
should glimmer such brilliant morning air
upon it's wings.

My Mother touched her face reflectively, as if
her own encircled eyes could change,
accept the curving yellow moon beneath their lids,
or that her skin could alter, become
a net of filaments to channel floating midnight.

Beyond my night-time window the owls
beck and hoop within the swinging stars.
There is a note they have that coos and churrs
gently as a dove-voice in the shadow trees.
A Goddess, once
held owls upon her arm for wisdom; perhaps to her
they used that throaty call of love.

If Owl Woman came to me, gold-winged
and wearing Mother's long rich dress,
we could go beyond the glass,
fly into the reaches of the cold October night –

and who would know
my colour burned as bright as sun itself
in daylight?
I'd fly like secret fire, if
she came to me.

WILD WOMEN

(Saturday Night at the Goddess Conference)

When Jana and Oshia sing
magic begins slow tempo stroking
my spine into snake and the snake-music
begins the go-round, rustles our skirts,
stirs the hair on the back of our necks –
kiss of Katrina's guitar on bare shoulders
of women dancing: cats of brocade,
green mermaids, silk horses. Lydia's drum
calls on the heartbeat, rhythm's footstep,
as voices ruffle black lace of Crow-
Mother, sigh in snowsleeves
of Owls lifting their wings beckoning Moon
cruising nightclouds. Hecate, Venus,
you and I stepping out in the song as it river-
roars through the throats of more singers – skins
jet/ honey/ amber/ pale alabaster – music rising
in the sweat of each note building
higher and higher scat and symphony
shaping a dancefloor out in the stars/
rainforest/ ocean – and we are all flying, wild
women free in their magical bodies – dancing.

THIS TIME, WE MAKE THE FIRE OF LOVE

(Goddess Conference, Glastonbury)

All around the wary town the gathered women
carry Lammas fire. It's in their pockets
and their little satin bags, small sparks innocent
as petals leaving spangles on the grass.
Some have rucksacks full of slithery flames that escape
in snaky tendrils down their backs, some
wear fiery sun-circles on their hands
rubies, garnets glint like darts.

The women carry fire in their bodies in red wombs
and red rivers, in young muscles full of kundalini grace,
in soft wrinkled skins brimmed with burning water;
and a hundred scarlet fireheaded women
set little bonfires bobbing in the street
so the town quivers at the dangers of ignition.

Light gives away only part of their secrets
in a gleam here and there, or that look, as if
within the eye's deep pool a goddess quickly
dazzled, and smiled as she lit the heart.

And these fiery loving women walk around astonishing
the tourists, the pilgrims and the town wives:
Of course, they say, of course we carry fire,
we have always done so: fire of Inanna, fire of Diana
fire of Bride, we are all sacred fireholders –
Hey lady – slip inside yourself and see.

MOTHER GOING OUT

for Oz

She was going out, dressed in spider-lace
black against pale skin, black
velvet gloves, black hat brim dipping down.
Her stiff black skirt whispered
hush and hush and hush
as she moved about my room, kissed me.
I am going out, little son, little best boy,
she told me as she drew her gloves
carefully down into the finger spaces
and pressed the silver bracelet's cuff
about her wrist. She was going out
maybe dancing, maybe not.

I watched the blissful fat white moon
sail over, the square below
was full of evening light and scuttling leaves.
I saw my mother's friends all come to meet her,
dark coats beneath the trees.
I leaned out, listened to their voices
skip and float amongst the oaks
like restless birds.
I saw her look up, smile to me
and then the crowd turned round
and each one raised her slow black arm
to wave goodnight. Their velvet hands were sleek
and sly as black cat's paws
and in the tricky, pearly moonlight I thought
their eyes reflected glimmering feline green.

BLACK WIND

for Katinka

There are nights that pluck at me
like witch-fingers, blood-sisters

I walk restlessly round the room
drink too much, tease, scold, scorn

I may tear something apart – tarot cards or flowers
but my hands are capable of crushing steel and bone

These are the nights when the black wind
flicks stars through the trees like elf-shot

when the black wind glides under my eyelids
so I own night-sight, am cat on the tiles

These are the nights when women shapeshift
fly and alight on a whim like a succubus

naked breasts cold as water, their hair
curled into snakes or spiked raven wings

These are the nights when everything cages me:
your gentleness, our love, the spaces between us

These are the nights, these nights of black wind
when you are best absent, your door closed

while I stay alone with my mirror sisters
watching the wind, the wild moon in my hand.

WOMAN WITH A SECRET ROOM

The woman with a secret room
does not speak of it even though her eyes
shine out whichever season, skyblue or
slategrey gold-flecked they shine out
yet this is not considered extraordinary,
no one remarks *look at that woman*
how she shines! She must be eating light!
Devouring whole electricity in sparking snakes
between the one negative pole of
her dark finger and the other positive pole of
her radiant day finger, dawn finger, sun finger.

She does not speak of it,
goes about her work, threads the spaces of crowds,
weaving, dancing lets money attend her
like leaves or rain or juggler's pieces;
is hooded as an owl: winter white furred in a tree
of waiting listening bones.
She has a coat like any other coat,
a webbing of thin wools, moorland and heather
mottled there as python   if she spins
in her coat, only the pavement and the stray dog
would attend to her spiral. Crazy Mother
winding her rags, her strings.

The woman with a secret room touches
as delicate as doe, or kitten, her fingertips
charge with love, children cluster, kiss.
Her lover closes his eyes and dreams and smiles –

These her dreams then:
the Wheel and Web Dream, the Dream of Love,

the Tree of Hope Dream, the Dream of Diamond Jaguar,
White Buffalo Woman's Dream. These run over her skin
their feet tattoo her, she is blood and colours,
the dreams prick sharp at her eyes, tears
flood her with water energy, running silk rivers
from her fontanel to her soles.

She has a black and white cat, milk on the step,
firecoal and mornings of old moon paleface
in the fragile sky, opposite weight to the sunrise.
She has a lock of delicate balance, a key of newborn gold.

LADY ARUM

Once, in a dry harbour where white arum lilies
rooted out of stones, salt and the old rusts of anchors,
there came a woman of such lightness
it seemed she was of material beyond our usual range,
her energy as different to ours as the blue
that comes off a swordblade is unlike
yet kin, to a knife's shined silver.

White Face owned a bell-voice, tongue-clapper calling
in the oval mouth of the lily.
*(You can watch it strike daily hours, that long black
tongue, rolling the sun, hitting the whiteness gently.)*
Her music slid subversively under the wave, seeped
through the hulls yawning and stretching in heavy heat.
It crannied into the pebbles and glittery shells,
into the urchin pools where crabs stared from viridian.
The guillemots listened, balancing slick rocks
backwards and forwards under their claws.

I thought the town would fall upside-down, people come
running, flapping ears like mad side-hats, hair kite'd.
I thought windows would fly with the force of opening
and chimneys flare with spontaneous flame. I thought
she and her honey would stir the whole hive of us,
always sleeping, eyes dazzled out and exhausted
by the cold intensive sea.

A space open in sky, an arch into somewhere other.
My hands were breast-stroking bracken that lavered the air
as seaweed, my boots were pollened. I blew gull notes
on a strand of grass –   and the arum lilies
licked salt from their chins, raised
their white faces over the curious waves that came

creeping to cover their leaves and feet, cover
their strong thighs, stems, singing throats.
Boats jostled uneasily, remembering forests. At eventide,

the light woman strolled across the harbour, humming.
And come nightfall, oddities of shadow squeezed like cats
from half-open doorways as one or two people,
huddled and grey in their furtive day-to-day coats,
entered her wagon. Each received a drum or a rattle,
and softly the lilies
                    began to beat time in a full circle.

SLEEPING AND WAKING

for Kathy

Some women walk the old paths in their midnight sleep
and sleepwalk through their daily trades
and their romances, deal with their hand-to-mouth monies
as if they were only ephemerals drifting past.
I know a woman who sleepwalks all the hours of her house
only waking when Wind comes from the West to take her
out of the skin of her this-world self.
Wind traces the spine of that self down her back
and the old self-skin falls like a cut coat
onto the bedroom floor as she walks away

through blossomed orchards and groves
of mossy oaks wide as gateways. Wind
rounding her ankles like a spaniel, lifting her hair
like a lover wanting the sweet nape of her neck.

She is awake then: to leaves susurration, their groaning
onto the quiet shoulders of rock, rock's monosyllabic answer.
She is awake to each plant's whitelight energy
streaming out of its stalk as she questions voices of water.
Horses follow her in friendship over fields where stars settle
hissing like snakes and white birds fly up in a snow
to tag the streamers of her spirit as she walks.
She is awake to her blood's fume and flow
and the needs of women for moonlight, as she begins
finding rituals again, waking the old paths in her wisdom:
making the healing prayer, the praisesong, the invocation.

LISTENING ELK-WOMAN

for Annie

Annie as Elk-Woman
could run through a thousand skies
white and gleaming, her eyes dreaming us all.

I love her rickety kitchen full of fetishes,
pictures, pinnacles of books, shelves
of crackle-flowered china.
She makes us salad with red-stalked chard,
listens to me grieve.
Outside a thrush sings in the cherry tree.

It is early summer. Annie's travelling
is showing through her skin, as if
bone and blood must be flooding now
with her desire to leap into Shamanka's forest
where secrets lie disguised as stones or roots.
She'll come back dancing stories,
casting antlered shadows. Every year
she's fiercer, understanding knives and hearts.

Still, she makes the salad, honey in the dressing.
She witnesses with wisdom and I hear her,
glad of friendship's consolation, friendship's
truthful shock. Outside, these later days
cherry tree is nodding, listening to her
with attention and the thrush has found some
English music for Elk's long-memoried song.

VISION OF THE REINDEER WOMAN

I am a woman of deerskin and fur, ice woman
fixed to the narrow heartbeat line
of the reindeer's diminishing pattern.
I am the hook, the hoop and the cauldron.
I walk with tongue-bright wolf and snarled wolverine.
I dream in the white blizzard's howl, dream
of the thousand ghosts of my broken drifting people.

This vision I saw:
black night creating a city of crystal;
sky's luminous feathers coalesced, froze
into tier upon tier of brightness, splintered ice towers,
arches of dazzle. Strange transparencies –
the colours name themselves into my mouth:
  Ruby: this is blood from the deer's throat
  flooding, connecting.
  Sapphire: bird-egg blue, delicate,
  twist of sun, snatch of sky-water.
  Amethyst: feast-smoke; friendship's
  heat on my lips.

The city is dreaming itself.
People appear on the first cold slopes,
their limbs pushing, swimming the glassy surface.
This bitter air cannot touch them; without fear
they are naked. Nor does the pure sensuous light
arouse them even as it touches radiance across
their different, awkward bodies. Their faces are quiet.
They climb with great purpose sometimes sliding back
or falling to space but always recovering, going on upward.
There is no returning.

I call to the reindeer across the snow.
The miners are near to this place, their tracks
gouging Earth, killing forever great swathes
of our delicate living. No moss will spring here.
We are few now and winter comes without land.
I will bear a child this solstice. These long months as I work
I have woven a spell of deer-fat and willow,
carved a horn amulet. I would have a daughter.
Let her climb beyond the dark.
For what will remain here, in this final, rich emptiness?

REMEMBERING NAN WADE
ON THE ISLE OF MAN

In the annals, a life becoming sentences:
Nan Wade came there and gave him herbs
to cure him. And a later date: *Nan Wade*
laid a word upon the child and she was whole.
Rumours of magic. Marks on paper, signatures
within a leaf: *this is lungwort, the spotted surface*
tells us of disease within that part, smoke-lesions
might look so blotched. Like to like it cures.
Stippled, spotted, each plant scrawled with messages
of veins, meridians, hand and eye and skin.

One old man, snowy stubble brushed raw
with burning poppy, remembering fire and storm:
I knew her! I'd seen St. Elmo's fire circling the rigging.
'You don't see it,' the men said. White-faced they were
always feared of marvels. And Nan Wade – a fellow
got a word from her and just one leaf he let go in the water.
Oh – that catch of herring nearly sank the boat!

Sun blazing silver of a million fish. Dangerous that leaf
To bring the fish with such a bible score.

And what leaf to cure a life lived at the edge?
In the frayed curl of a fern, seed small enough
to clench the rune that makes invisible; bracken
hedging an unobtrusive house, neat enough not
to draw attention to the twilight girls,
to nightshade, henbane, leopardsbane.
A prayer for silence; no word of mouth
conniving at a blame – *They burn them here*
in barrels wild as hell, a blazing spinning fire
descending with the hag.

I'll keep tidy, go to church, say yes, yes, yes.
Memory plays strange tricks in places such as this.

The healer always watching for the supernatural warning
in the masts of yew trees or village oaks, always waiting
for the suppressed aerial violence of the thunderstorm
to break about her head in iron hoops of fire.

PRECOGNITION

They told me how you almost sang your predictions,
extolling the praises of each future's web, the lines
held in the hand. Seek her, they insisted,
rosy with your safe reading, slotted in
between therapy, analysis.
Go learn the hour of life's improvement.
They were so sure of your prognosis.

Yet it was also whispered that your voice could fall,
take on the guttural timbre of a man's
– some soul-lost gypsy speaking in your mouth.
            That was dangerous,
when the words arc'd and buckled, heaved flatly
from your lips like small blind imps.
But in the ordinary way of it your voice made no mutation.
You were soothing, there was nothing to fear
in your cheap brown rooms where china horses
grazed tranquil on glass shelves.

It was difficult to breathe, some days.
Alone at my cold window
fears fell on me like snow. So I came to find you,
catching at the least straw in my consuming wind.

And for me you had put on robes.
I entered a place of conjuration where black silk on the walls
negated daylight and the pinned lepidoptera of tarots, zodiacs,
fluttered warnings chill as seeds of ice. Your tannined fingers
scuttle on my palm, your inward eyes pick and stare,
uncaring of what ghosts and pasts inhabit me.
It is the divination of my tomorrows that will make you burn.

The awkward bass discord of your speech holds no surprise.
I already knew that even had you used some other voice
the sentence would have been the same.

ONLY MAID

From Captain Rostron of the Carpathian to George E.Foster,
Acting Premier Ottowa, April 18th 1912,
after the wreck of the Titanic
'Isidore Strauss and wife not on board, only maid.'

We were sleeping   I had a cot in her dressing room
more space for her furs than for me but life was soft –
curled like a kitten
into the sleeve of her Chinese kimono
Mari, you do my hair so fine, she said

Jesse said my hands loved the feel of things
glass, linen, lace, organza, red hair –
when the brush rippled lamplight like cat's paws over the lake.
Her hairbrush was silver-backed turtle, heavy as lead

Startling awake I lay with fear opening me
into a great stillness, a nought, a nothing, a space –
then clamour washed over me and I called out their names
and we ran and collided and fell and we clung
and we struggled, scrabbled for clothes and I saw
Mr Strauss snatch up a necklace
but it broke into drops as we watched –
rained slow rubies into the dark
that I hauled the big sealskin out of the rack
and folded it carefully around her
 her hair was wild with sleep and sweat
lying like waterweed, flat tendrils over her nape

 I was running uphill in crowded blackness and no one
was real anymore. We were all grey shadows and bones
we were unstrung rubies, drums, we were fists made of iron
hearts turned to ice

We crouched so quiet, I and those strangers;
someone wrapped mink round my shoulders
tiny shrill paws of mink plucking and praying
swinging to/fro in the rocking motion

I soothed the fur with my hands, whispered comfort
as Time closed its silence over us all
and called us to witness how stars were salted down
into the water and shone in the eyes of the dead
like a handful of pearls spilt over the sea

MORGAN'S BOAT

Always this idea of the royal barge, the stately ship
moving quietly through calm darkness, three Queens
containing his bitter death between their trinity.
We knew they shared healing skills, something sung
beyond those sour elixirs of betony, burnet, chesnut,
Time's lines threaded zodiacs on their silky palms.
Three Queens crafting a great barge across a space
of shadows; the King's broken body smoothed straight
that he might lie in grace.

So it was told.
How three Queens came for Arthur and took his dying,
solemnly; the blackened world hushed down
to the sound of a boat gentling through water.
So history has it.

But when Morgan came to him she was mad with grief
for the stars had fallen with him and he lay
in a welter of such deep burning
she thought the land would split asunder.
She chanted his body with lines searing electric blue
into his gaping wounds, she demanded the bones of rock
out of their loamish sleep to use their augeries
- *old dreams took up stations under the oaks,*
orchards grieved fearful immediate autumns, tumults
of apples falling fire-signs out of the dark.
She summoned Westwind and her ship of glass;
in her arms – she striding air her feet never touching –
he was a slight limpness, the husk of the grain.
In her boat he lay on the boards with his broken head,
his opened head in the red cauldron of her lap.
She called her sisters to come and they came leaping
black feathers flying down from the thundering crags,

hurled power down from their wintering mountain;
all they could grab with both hands before
cut-throat cold savaged in from the East.

So Morgan watched
the bloody messed body that was her brother
and she turned her dragon engines towards Avalon.
Cutting the water like a sword, she made full speed.

SILK PAINTING PRAYER FOR RAIN

The nature of the dragon is rough and fierce,
Li Shi-Chen said, his hands gold brushing
dragon scales. These are sensual movements.
He is Life, tail-in-the-mouth and such spiked wheel
to churn plain weathers into cyclic fire.
Li Shi-Chen paints his costly pigments
lapidary on silk, feels the lux of azurite
flute liquid in his veins as he records
the recent ceremonial prayer for rain.
His finished scroll will open only
for expensive private meditation.

That which pleases him
is ruby. Also the water-hearted Stone of Darkness.
He may eat that, take it
between his long wild-bearded lips so gently.
Li Shi-Chen whistles softly through his teeth;
lets the marvellous silk pour across his arms
like water, or her black unbounded hair.
This texture warms his heart. He quickens.

And the catalogue of fears, Li Shi-Chen tells her.
They tremble at the sight of iron or centipedes,
fear the leaves of wang and lien, fear
silken thread of binding five-spice colours.
Li Shi-Chen's lips make tastes appear, star anise
and pepper; he spreads morsels with his tongue:
This is cassia, these are cloves and fennel,
suck and see. Dragons wish to feed forever
on the dainty aromatic flesh of roasted swallows.
Li Shi-Chen understands desire. Equates it
with a burning need to slake his thirst.

The dragon has nine resemblances.
She remembers: *horn of stag, burning eye of demon.*
Obedient, she lies still as well-water
as she tells the painter: *I heard his angry screaming*
as they kept him from me. A weird sound,
like thin striking of a thousand copper basins.
She remembers rough ceremonial silk beneath
her nakedness, the dominant jade focus of the sky.
Priest and acolytes watching, allowing only
the dragon's sudden potent storm to touch.

Li Shi-Chen's clouds engorge with promise.
The girl is strewn amongst other sorceries,
tiger bone and ash. The summoned dragon hovers rain
above the ritual of temptation. Li Shi-Chen smiles,
bruises oyster for the moist sheening of her skin.
This day, she does not pray for rain.

RAINBOW DAY

Just another autumn Monday.
I swept the stony floor, cleared cat hairs
from the sofa, dust motes like smoke
in my dry throat.   *Oh these works –*
I give thanks for the child
who songbirds me through my finicking kitchen
and scorched brassica garden.

But the sky made a sudden change to new harmony
bluegrey with thunder, and a gilding trick
painting sunfire on yarrow, mugwort, old lupins,
throwing purple to shadows, leafgold against
mock-April blue or a bruising lilac –
rain wilding down from the dark frowning west,
the east glittering azure and rainbowed.

I danced the bow,
the rain, the sun, the whole weather,
the bright wet firing of roof and leaf,
stone and grass-blade, I danced them:
left foot leaping
with wrist go round and head shake,
I made the stamp stamp of the oak,
sang the bell-toned apple and yammering damson
as I danced the rainbow into the Earth.
Let the bow bring seeds and rivers,
birds and babies and colours,
let the rain wash us clean as beginning
I danced, water-dressed, drenched, shivering.

Then I coaxed the fire,
cooked the evening's aubergines
with garlic, coriander, a twist of orange.

I turned the sheets about, kissed the child's scratches
and curled my amazing agile long black legs lazily
onto the sofa, while I read *The Honeycomb*,
and allowed the moon to come hand over fist
up to my open window.

RAINDANCE

Water is a woman with long hair
who stands at the crossroads of deserts
to offer the liquid cup of her mouth
to all comers, strangers, children.
She is a woman whose clean black throat
is a gateway to brilliant stars,
a woman whose tides flow through her sisters.
She is the healing tongue,
the secret drowned sleep of the dreamers.

Come Water-women, thin as pipes, fat as lotus,
come and dance, dance the water down:

Woman-Cool-as-White-Wine, Woman Lie-in-the-mud,
Surf-rider Woman, Snake-river Woman,
Storm Woman, Steamy Woman, dance
dance the water down;
Lake-lily Woman with gold skin,
Mermaid Woman of Pearl, come dance the water down.
Woman with big brass taps, faucets and showers,
Woman with fountains of tears,
           Red Moon-woman, Milk-Woman, Juice-Woman –

           all Waterfalling Women
dance, raindance the sacred water down.

WEST COUNTRY FARMER'S MARKET

Always early, we crowd into concrete halls
and even after disappointment in love, too much rain,
fear of climate change and money – we smile:
there is a good dream here, some new created light.

It comes in the form of buttocky pumpkins
bright as a laugh, in a tumble of scarlet peppers,
Pippins, polished brownskin shallots reflecting
exchanges; in knobbled beets or cabbage
– a finery of black plumes laid in a careful box.
It's in the dark smell that crumbles dirty in our fingers
when we heft potatoes, it's in the reek of saltweed fish,
line-caught from the leaping blue. It's in hen-memory:
red loam under rosebush and witchy elder, every egg
a solar universe. It's in the magic of fresh beans,
green and purple fistfuls of shiny beads fizzing my lips
to sensation, crunch-raw or garlicky, fine-herbed
with thyme my tongue remembers from heights of larksong;
orchards, summerlands laid out below in their green promise.
It's in the given craft – handmade bread fit to break fast
with saints at their cliff-top refuge, flung spume
for seasoning, a feast with honey and ewe's cheese
gleaned from the rich Levels, small, sweet breathing fields.

This good dream is the way it was when we understood
the turning world and our connection within it,
touching joy. This good dream is how it will be,
from now on: our mouths, minds, hearts and hands, honest;
spirit farming our earth, shaping this cradle
to hold the dreams of our children's children.

DOMESTIC GODDESS

It is not in the instances of chocolate parfait
that I become a Domestic Goddess,
nor within the *bain-marie* nor the couscous.
          No, rather it is in the spaces
after housework – the kind that comes
three weeks late and shows in low sun's freight
of dust motes like stellar atoms
suspended in a dance over dulled furniture
                    – in these spaces
when my orderliness has polished the shine
into goldframes and chestnut surfaces,
when china sings with all its mouths
clean and wide open as nests full of thrushes
and glass celebrates itself in mirrors of light
then –when I am alone
and float through the presences of every room
blessing things gently – this clock of ages,
these pages and sweet cakes
                    then I grow tall and svelte
dress in rivery silvery gowns and stilettos
make my mouth a wild luscious mulberry
trail musk over the windows in veils
and trap the street sounds like flies for slaughter
so the bright silence will sing me
and you will respond
in each room's bloom and dizziness
will bow and give thanks and follow me
into the white linen sanctum upstairs
where the windows are wide to the oak spires
and birds robed as black priestesses, sing praise.

MAPPING THE BORDERS

At the river   water and evening light
are gathering unknown colours,
a skin of desire   unsayable as blue hill mist.

    So much collects for me here:
in the folds of woods
    my mothering arms (these trees are grown now
        as tall as my son and daughters),
   I am the brook listening intently to music,
I am strix in the winter garden beyond the bright window,
saying the song over and over, charmed by response.

    The grace of this land – rain-scud
across rounded fields, red furrows angled at an edge,
hedge crab apples, bracken left loose for adders –
holds me: breathless, stranded.

      Something happened to me here.
I found the axle of my world that brought me round to this:

love turns me still. All this familiar landscape is praise.

FAITHS

You are looking for something to recognise
but the altar is recessed in darkness, black cave-mouth
roaring and smoking with gilt and incense

Saints stare plaintively out, bleeding from the powers
of their silvers and oil and jewels; like survivors
we stumble into the courtyard of wide white air

high as the lammergeiers; there is one pomegranate tree
dressed like a dancing woman in fire-red silk:
skirts deep enough to burn your lips.

At Armeni you photograph me under the kerm oaks:
I am a priestess serving the spirits with my hands
of dry leaves and jade lizards.

You lean down to take the picture from me as I stand
in the stark angle of the dromos; in the shadow behind me
the Goddess is axle, stone pillar of light.

You retreat to wait on a bank of wild narcissus
where you are Pan, playing gospels on your pipe
careful as a Jain of the small lives of beetles

as you talk to the goats in the same soft chattering
swooping bird-speech that the lemon-leaf-gathers
call to each other across the groves.

I feel the breath of the cold stones at my back as beautiful.
When I turn round, the sun itself
is your kiss on the nape of my neck.

SHAMANKA

Under the acrid smoke
the dreams were leaping and binding,
trailing their sensuous breath
as watered silk: scarved wolf in the grey,
hackled fox, owl-shadow, secret
oblique lynx; all gathering.

White moon-face, listening slant, she
entices the drum to enter the slender bowl
of her bones; strong thighs
gripping the bucking music,
the rattle of nerves.

To the cage of her flickering wrist
the leopard is called from the shadows.

I swear! her arms grew furred and maculate
as she began the ascension: going out with the smoke
through the space of the pole star,
into the void.

If I lost you
I would sing the drum,
stretch naked for great mottled cats
to inhabit my skin; let my eyes fold inward.
I'd find you, hold: though the spirits
were dancing the feast of your soul,
I would journey the shallow entrancing skies
with feather bone fire –
bring you back home.

GREAT RIVER

Nothing is ever lost, no inheritance ever broken.
The tree does not die in the leaf,
matter is only one manifestation of energy;
within the fernseed lies desire
for invisibility, within the aconite
a dream of flight.
So witches touched the stars; women black
as cormorants, chanting spirals with closed eyes.

All is connected, there is no edge
between Time or Space.
I touch the furthest reaches, go beyond
the glassy lens into the unrimmed places
where star's dark companions watch.
Undiscovered countries;
reaching them is as easy and as difficult
as placing my lips against your inner arm.

This touch: knowing the archaic stellar dust
within the tremor of your pulse, here in the wrist
where your veins run rivers, life channelled,
circular, spiralling fine threads
more delicate than Spiderwoman's web.

Picture the Great River
flowing with Souls, with Bodies of Light,
fugitive colours earthborn in the dark:
atoms of red ochre, ultramarine.
How do we dream, accept divinity within us?
Our breath is Air, we are flowing elements,
we are the promises of stars.

Sunset dims, the room charms with shadow,
changes come. Now this fleeting moment
is thick and soft, dark
breathing animal velvet about us,
night within the walls.
We prove the edgelessness of matter, merge
our sheened bodies. Bright constellations
are the nub of your spine, Egyptian eye,
your willow mouth spinning laughter
further than Andromeda.
Look-   when I hold up my hands
light streams skyward out of my fingers
links us into the journeying Silver Wheel above.

VENUS

Green dawn and Venus rises over black lace oaks,
sleep's kingdom of shutters and ceilings.
In some earliness she is huge, earthy,
the eye of a fire-drake shining deep in the strength

and rock of her but today she is all sharp lights,
a child's star-drawing, a burning snow-crystal
containing the heat and heart of her radiance:
her prophecy of love.

I open the door on my dreaming mound
invite her to enter. I am used to stepping outside,
within, into other – but this is different –
I swing the space open to allow her to enter: here.

And find that up-close she is all White Fire Goddess
as she hurtles into the room with electricity
violent as planetary birth, storm force
licking up corners and edges, making explosions

- lights that crackle and jump, scintillate,
through my peonies and marcasite necklaces
as she flies into my heart to send me sky high
with such love I am opened wide as heaven.

Her flame in my eyes, I turn away from the window
to watch you sleeping beside me, still in the world
of linen and clocks. I wait – patient for only a moment –
before I wake you with the first of my fire-raising kiss.

WORKING WITH SNAKES

This girl, paces the school corridor, a snake
on a pole held before her. This house,
has arched it's cold stone crenellated back,
is a creature ready to strike, drawn breath
hissing, the high closed windows squinting
the last red sun down the slope
of the polished hall, where the girl
with the smooth snake is walking softly,
her sandals tapping softly, Snake
in a green curl ringing her stick.

Light is scarlet through glass as
the dining-room door snaps open and girls pour out
in a stream that breaks and shatters
into ring within ring of high piercing yelling
round Snake's quicksilver turning –

SNAKE SNAKE SNAKE!

This girl at the still centre:
as the nuns come running towards me
their hair stiffening, skirts sharpening –
fingers that rules lines, lines that will never be snake
with life coiling and quick eyes, flicking tongue.
They are coming – converging straight down the chaos
of girls laughing and leaping – all the dry women
are drawn into the line and the loop
of my pole and my prize, my marvel,
while I stand with Snake
twisting, circling the stick to keep it
caught in the tension.
But look, it's marvellous, a grass snake! Beautiful!

They are pointing their cursing fingers –

Sharp in the child, the rod, the ruler, the backbone
straight as a law. The women are rattle-bones
clicking and snapping, the die is cast.
I carry Satan, Worm, the Great Contaminator,
the Dragon whose harm coiled round the hills
and wound through the caves and rivers.
Snake is masculine/feminine, pushing
its bright head forward, thrusting, seeking
the safe dark of the hole it fits so smoothly.

Snake's death is certain.
No escape into the cool rivulets of grass
or through a secret labyrinth of stone.
Snake must have its brains strewn
across a wall in a wild and ugly letting,
sending its spirit to coil appalled above my head.

Listen to me, dry ladies of the past,
I have made a long reparation to Snake.
I have discovered for myself it's sinuous dance,
its vital energy that moves in secret through
the world's landscapes, fusing all the darkness
of the inner earth with flowing water, fire and air.
I have made a home for Snake within me
where Snake is busy: from the touch of fingers on my lips
it has made a fig tree blossom in my bones;
Snake's coils are my body's contours
when my lover understands them with his hand,
Snake's suppleness is the river of my limbs
becoming liquid when I cleave to love.
And when my lover enters, I am Snake
with lightning tongue, licking flames
that lie like suns along his spine –
their radiance wraps us, so we fly through light.

But look, it's marvellous, a grass snake! Beautiful!
This girl walking softly, trees summer-heavy,
air gentle, river flowing over rocks.
I am watching the snake's long slither through sunlight,
its gloss and power, curious quicksilver circling,
returning to the safe dark mazes under the earth.

PROMETHEA

She dressed carefully: gloves of asbestos and kicking shoes,
black shadow leotard. She let her hair fall from its band
shook it out to a frizzed electric circle,
kindled her lips red

    Close to, near the rim
a hut of black leaves, black air a swathe of chiffon
over eyes, mouth and breath. For days
she sat in the chime of the place, allowing the hours
to swing slowly past; metronomic, subtle as weather.
She found the rift on the sixth count
        where the quick indrawing – *for what milk*
or what honey – opened a split-second slit
        and she slipped inside.

Corridors in a ruled maze; intersections, trivias,
and at their edges, water in gleaming runnels
        echoing different music
under the great heart beating ignition into each cell.

Cat-padding softly, steel-tips clicking like claws
or the secret opening of locks, she went from shadow
to shadow, her hair a placating illusion of smoke.

She expected the single store: box and disc.
But realised it was in the wires, every connection
linked in a web fine as her own hair, long as the world.
        Oiled, slick with nerves
and practice, she inserted the keys of her fingers
her thoughts, her own named crystals   and felt
the whole creation shock through her.

Numberless, mathematical, and she could not count
could not count the tiers of burning stars
nor the unfolding precision of black distance
the etch of fire in her mind:
     I am fragile, I am afraid, I am a seed in space
        She pulled out, hands hurt and heart
 nearly stopping into the fall

and saw again, how the water in every trackway
ran with light: the mercurial grace of light on water,
connecting   – spring, creek, channel, river, estuary
into the radiant Ocean – the same fire:

so this is my beginning
her own veins and great arteries carrying the spark.

NIGHTFIRE

I am moving towards Death
on feet of flame.
        Fire ripples over my skin
as soft as kisses
I am radiant   inside out
fire   crazing my keen surfaces
        melting the glaze
from my old self   my veneer and finish.

        I am a bowl of fire.

There are moments at night
when if I walked naked into the sea
I would plume light, my body phosphorous, ruby
  I would be Giant
Fire Woman blazing   in joy
     allowing nakedness through and through.

Water flows: dew forms, on my back, on my lip.

Moon is complicit   accepts:
I am not perfect   I am small, old, my skin
        a drooping silk in moon's beam,
    I let go   let go.

And I am a fiery angel   crouched
on Jacob's ladder with flame-feathers blazing
out of my heels and over my head, brightening
the mouth of the dark   as I wait to ascend.

INANNA GIVES LAPIS LAZULI

So Inanna went to the black gate
and gave her lapis lazuli necklace
into wraith hands. Breastplate, crown,
her pala-garment of woven eastern silk
were taken from her and she was naked.

Up in the far lands, a lark is singing;
we drink coffee, make love. We live in a time
of terror, joy and sorrow, a fragile peace
made with the Universe.

In the Abyss, Inanna rotates slowly on the hook
like meat, like meat. Wise Ereshkigal
watches her sister's eyes cloud over
as she enters death; *salt tears, bitter blood,*
this season seems a winter caught in stasis

Our blue planet wears a royal beauty
before the deepest night, before the dawn.
Inanna, let me remember, how after the Abyss
you returned in wisdom, adorned with lapis lazuli
and silk: a Queen with fierce, blazing eyes.

THE SOURCE

They have taken the soft birds from under her breasts
cut the blue roots out of her veins.
They stood inconsequentially talking of meat and money
while they peeled away the skin of her arms
where the tongues of deer and bear were recorded.
They dusted their poisons into her spaces, let her bees
fall out in a firestorm. They cut back her hair
and singed her scalp so nothing will grow there now
no green horses, no lianas, no lizards, no babies.
They drank the water out of her eyes, dammed
the silver water table in concrete so she stares blankly

but the tears still come.

No one can quench the source of the river under the river
and myths and dreams and healing still flow out of it.
We know she lives. She is the voice of the newborn
and the Ancestor, the gaze of the last white tiger
and the flower that breaks through the road.
She is the red thread of life in all of us;
she is tomorrow and we cry for her: *Mother, free us.*

HUNTING SILENCE

The hunters have set lime on every branch,
put nets of mist across the evening sky
so birds that wheel the world each year and dance
the sun around, will pause to rest, and die.
The Wind is keening loss. He has no freight,
no featherweight to carry home to groves
where nightingales would wake him, sleeping late,
or larks rise singing praise to vine and rose.
The birds will turn to Wind and sigh his name:
Wing! Go! Their songs are stone, their tongues are dry,
they fall from breath: each death a little game;
each singing heart is pinned and cannot fly .
The land lies shocked, brutalised by silence:
the loss of song itself, immense violence.

*Note: In Cyprus, limed sticks, mist-nets and semi-automatic
rifles are used to illegally hunt an estimated 20 million
migrating birds each Autumn.*

STORM TIGER

for Storm

Someone has taken the tiger away
from my friend's small daughter. Someone
has sneaked thick hands into the forest (*forests of rain,
forests of clouds flowers lichen) lifted the tiger out like a toy.*
Now they are plucking the hairs from its pelt one by one
letting them drift through tomorrow's sky, a mist
of fine gold-plated needles, gold shimmer in air only seen
in the equation of angles of sight with your distance,
your own losses, your knowledge of Lords of Light.
Each hair is precisely the length of a logged tree:
so many million trees stacked by the river, jostling
forests of tigers silting the rising brown waters.

The black bars on the pelt re-phrase as a sorrow-song.
Someone has spent a lifetime – or more? *How many
lifetimes, laid beginning to end ? Enough
to fracture the history of dreams or a continent's heart
come loose from its mooring in mangroves and orchid –*
a lifetime tearing the skins of tigers, flensing their bones,
stripping each penis down to an old man's mouthful of vigour.
Someone nailed tiger-power to a tree, slit cold golden stares
into skulls that haunts forever. Someone slips skin
under skin, strokes draped coats of curved fur over thin bones,
blood sealed out of seams smearing red across lips and fist.
Someone's hands are gold-dusted (as a tiger half seen in sunset)
palms scored with life-lines of deals, stains no rains
will wash away, marking forever the promise of zero.

My friend's daughter has a soft cartoon of a tiger, affable mouth,
a long tail to express endearing emotion, paws that are fingers
easily asking for more, glass eyes yellow as butter.
She kicks it over the pool and leaves it slumped on the concrete,

a splayed straw thing, a cheat that would trap her
with cheap velveteen. At five years old she dreams she is Tiger,
green as viridian frog and forest grass, stalking something
she can't yet name. She'll run on silently, searching through years
and midnight yards, over fences, roads, her shadow huge cat
on the city walls, fluid with wild grace, with anger: a Storm.

FIELD OF LIGHT

If I grieve for the loss of this bright field,
for this small water-vole in the silver river,
for this frail and ancient tree of life, this place
of ordinary light   and if in grieving
know all these will find their deaths – as I too –
in the void that is Her darkness, Her mystery – if
I cherish grief as carefully as I cherish love, then

I can trust to *not-knowing*. I can put my soul
to the work of singing the bones back into the future
of sometime, someplace: honoured, loved, whole –
even changed into beauty beyond all recognition.

BECAUSE

Because the world is being broken
into allotments of dollars and loss
we will plant our fruit trees and lilies
in the cracks between paving stones.

Because the world is rinsed scarlet with blood
we will take our own reds of passion and heart
and place them in hearths and love's look
knowing their potential for healing fire.

Because the world's spirit is being torn
we will mend our own webs of connection,
that fine lace, stretching between us
connecting us into all life, in every direction.

Because the sky is being clouded over
with smoke and dirt and armoured stars
we will stand in the dark of mountains,
in backstreet alleyways and in deserts

to call out the old names of the starry ones,
the sky dancers: *Astarte, Arianrhod, Venus, Aditi,*
our eyes shining, our eyes shining with hope.

THE FIELD

I want the field to be good for nothing
except itself.

I want the field to be random,
exploding with glittering spider gauze
or studded with swoops of starling
in their black sudden chatter and fizz, then gone.

I want the field to delight in its giving,
offering owlsong to night, honeysuckle's sweetness
to summer shadows hock-deep under oaks,
a stream's rest and deliverance.

I want the field to care;
to shuffle itself around to make space
for new calves, a million beetles, thousands
of buttercups, a hundred bees, slink foxes,
picnics, two May cuckoos.

I want the field to be green with
clover and plantain and orchid and selfheal –
not emerald with ryegrass and nitrogen.

I want the field not to have to prove anything
by statistics of wheatweight.
I want the field to have its own quota
of roe deer, walkers, horses, flies, vetch.

I want the field to be able to borrow a free month
of bright dresses – chicory, moonflowers, poppies,
hedges of damson, cherry-snows, dog-roses.

I want the field to work honestly
striving each season to fullness
of hay or beets or corn, its hedges weaving
a winter-living of berries, thoughtfulness of hazels.

I want the field to have wild times
and grace notes, fallow dreams.
I want the field to be cherished, loved as family.
I want the field to be good for nothing except itself.

PRAYER FOR ALWAYS PEACE

I ask all the animals to open their mouths
to howl this prayer for peace

I ask all the birds to lift their songs to the winds
and sing this prayer for peace

I ask all the trees and flowers, all that is green growing
to open their hollow throats where the sap runs
to call this prayer for peace

I ask the rocks to dream this prayer for peace

I ask the sand to rearrange its grains
and write this prayer for peace

I ask the ocean wave to shout this prayer for peace
or whisper it on the lonely listening beaches
where the rivers will send it upstream
in the willing breath of fish

I ask the deep wells to give rise to this prayer for peace

I ask the holy hills to toll this prayer for peace

I ask the stars to shine the spelling
of this prayer for peace

and the moon and the sun pause in the sky
as night and day, as right and left, as east and west
as all that is opposite yet may still come into balance
in harmony with this world, and in time

I ask for every candleflame to ignite this prayer for peace
so that this prayer is in the world and of the world
and becomes the world and the world is peace.

PRAYER FOR REMEMBERING THE EVENING, THE SEA, THE POSSIBILITIES OF SHADOW, LIGHT

Lady, I see how the great clouds go
sailing through this blue wind, grant this for me:
that I remember how the light changes.

Grant that I may keep this awareness
of the world's veils and layers –
cumulous and the coursing air
close here, salt on my skin and the white swan's curve;
And space - beyond, at the back of the wind
in this warm October still the evening sky opens
a gateway that is cerulean as May.
The stars will enter here,
are already hovering at the halo'd edge of sight.

Grant that I may always hold the vision
of how light-beings dance gold
on the rim of distant mountains lying soft as smoke.
Of how grey fragments the hems
of stately pyramids floating radiant amber,
or streams in silver between the rays of blessing-rivers
that flood the west horizon halfway home to Ireland.

The mist collects and balances the shadows of the hills,
fills with light to lay a rainy opal skein across the sea.
    Lady, I thought I saw dolphins out there –
their bodies singing in the dim curling of the wave –
Grant that they swim, surface in silent midnight
and that I, waking on the soul's dark journey
may remember
this evening: the rising moon,
the sea's glittering voice and race,
the possibilities of shadow and of light.

PRAYER TO LIVE WITH PARADOX

I want to be young in wonder again,
to hold a single seed to the sky and marvel
that it owns the energy of a star. I want to
be grown big enough for my vast protective arms
to encompass whole rainforest miracles
of tree-dazzle, life-power. I want to be light
as a leaf on the earth. I want to be the weight
that carries promise-flowers to fruit, greens
Darfur to peace and nurtures Lebanon's vineyards
through all four seasons gift to eye and tongue.

I want to learn the use of grief that honours those
creature-spirits who leave us, that long, on-going
shadow-procession: Nightjar and Loggerhead,
Gold-ringed Tanager, Arabian Gazelle,
Yellow-shouldered Blackbird, howler monkey,
Hyacinth Macaw and salamander, sea mink
forever swimming to horizons beyond the blue –

I want to learn the use of joy in those who stay,
somehow still keeping faith in the family of humankind:
cranes and sweet horses, rainfrogs and mountain lizards,
Bald Eagles, elk and caracal, Mexican Spotted Owls
thriving on the rooftops of Los Alamos, chaffinch
in the lilacs, coyote, otter, Golden Jackal; huge herds
of shining white-eared kob running on the sands
of South Sudan, parakeets thriving wild in London –

So much I want, a whole world I want – yet want
nothing without first serving World's want and need.

RUNNING ON EMPTY

I ran from my Mother before I was born
(and she'd tried so hard, made me of star-ash, clay, rain)
but I raced downtown and went chasing the easy speedy
routes over fields of fuel (feet dirty, heart hungry)
trawling the wide mouth of my Fendi sack for spoils,
discarding and trading: *uranium, copper and cotton,*
bodies and palm oil, sugar, coffee, coal futures, gold –

Someplace I spilled babies, somewhere I drew crowds,
but I rushed on faster, eating and spitting out riches,
winding higher and higher through wasteland and mountain
until I reached the edge and stopped – with nothing before me.

Sirocco and shadow have formed the last of my family:
Grandmother Earth, stick-thin and bony, so fragile, so
easily broken; scorched, hairless, dry breasted, abraded –
Only the two of us matter, only us in existence.

I could leave her. Go on running on empty –
or take off my Prada jacket and wrap it around her,
set tinder to flame in my shoes and sit at her feet, listening
to Wisdom: the First voice of Spirit, breath of the future.

SEDNA AT TADUSACK

Fierce Dark Salt Mother

I dreamed that Sedna stood up out of the ocean
skyscraper high, bright as the sun, glassy
with white sea flowing and falling to dress her
in blue fathoms, green powers and silvers.

She held up her apron of living water
and in it, this spit of land, the long wide river,
the whales that curve through the tide
all lay at peace in their day's work and her love.

Sedna cherishes this rare place where Pattern
is woven by working between light on the waves
and the land, between dark's deep indigo, stars
and whales' cold cycles of song; between peoples.

Sedna, care for us all. Even though we wring the sea
 dry with our nets, teach us in time to reweave
the World Pattern, so all oceans, all lands and peoples
may balance together, in the sling of your deep sea love.

THE CAILLEACH

The Cailleach walks violently over the winter's hills
and faraway, coming ever closer and closer
in a white tracksuit and seven white furs;
Dark Goddess tramping winter in her silver boots.

She says *cold for the time of year*
and pretends to be mild, slapping her arms around herself
and smiling her foxy smile under her wolverine skins.
The heads of her furs bob and rattle their skeletons
like rainbeads, their eyes glint, knowing black crystal.

If she shakes her furs close to your head you get white noise
and inability to think. This will lead you into the dream so
you'll forget where your feet are – even in ice –
and start seeing images flowing at the back of your eyes.
Some will be blunt and scary; old shadows
made by a big hand on the wall and not animals, not animals
that time locked deep in the frozen safe of your skull.

But you can learn to fly here. Climb first
through the hard rocks and hurts of her ankles, crawl over
her overhung knees and cling on for dear life
as you scale the cold glass of her ice-mountain thighs;
these heights will swing round you like some old bull-roarer
screaming of thunder and your fall.
Enter her dark river valley; follow the secret track of moss
and reindeer to her spring; her water inside your mouth
is the fire heart of crystal. Rest –
you will be smaller than one single snowflake as you cross
the sheer storm-scarp of her belly.

At her breasts, you will be on your knees in swan-feathers.
If you pass the hollow oak of her neck and her vulpine grin,

if you pass her look and go into the high steep whiteness of her –

she will let the air separate for you, allow you
to fly   a white hawk from her wrist
looking down on the long, fearful journey you have made

and the beginning
of tomorrow's new, terrifying, marvellous path.

GRACE

How I fear the ice that comes like a midnight thief
to smother my heart when cold winter
is more than weather and Time is snapped in its stalk.

Old Winter: the two-faced woman who bears such
deathly features and such grace as she walks
towards me, comes to turn my unwilling face to her gaze

and I see the world shrink to the target's eye, gold hawk
flung in a fire to raze all the patterns that are beautiful,
so we are lost. Our futures as poor as dust.

In this hour Vixen creeps from the hole, screams
her nightmare song in my dream of tomorrow stark
as snow, a long forever white-out without kindness.

But she is singing the coming months into new life
and being wholly alive, grace is as necessary as the flow
of blood or water. I listen: Winter marks me, makes me

know that in the terror of loss, the iron seizure of frost –
grace still holds strong as light: fox-star in the dark.
Believing then in grace is good enough: is grace itself.

INTO THE DARK

The Autumn trees have made a firedance
to take us down into the dark.
Lit torches of red maple, burning chestnut,
fiigree leaves of gilded yellow birch
attend our spiral path with flame
as we step below dry drifts of gold
to reach the place of granite black,
the starless space where Ceridwen stalks
black winds and holes and hollows.
Reaching in, she warms her hands
at heart's bright fire and ignites the night
with spirits – winged, wise-eyed and wild.
At her side, the Ancestors are patient,
their fingers stretch towards us –
nearly touch
black on black divisions fall to nothing.
Ceridwen walks between the radiant trees
and speaks the word that sets them weeping;
from her open mouth the Winter whistles,
again, she's making changes: she's crow
and winter barley, she's the cold rain
creeping in. Within her hand she holds
our memories of those who went before us,
one by one descending to the starless dark.

WINTER ASCENSION

The day star has quickened
and heavenly blue
comes in the winter afternoon
                    falls softly
around my shoulders
                    like a cloak.
        Beauty
takes my hand to walk me
into the deceits of darkness
that lie between my courage
and my release in Spring.

Old Cailleach grinds her teeth
 and drops black ash and poisoned water
            across the face of Earth
            that'll teach you!
            your heart is burdened,
                    embers dead with sorrows
                    as the star descends.

        Darkness is attended here – cloaked, cowled,
        ghostly – in shadows, curtains shut
        across the sun
                    as Time slows down

        ancestral bones come sleek and sharp
        within the land, caves open out like flowers

        and the star slows, settles now
            to the final ache
                of the long fall
            go deep now, breathe it in

this moment, know the raven-dark
of death.
Tomorrow
light shoots a thousand ways
and something new is born
within the starshell of the solstice.

No darkness now can be as grievous
as the hours of yesterday –
for this brief season.

This is ascension time –   sing!
Let the light hold you through the ice.

NOVEMBER LIGHT

November light silvers black trees and rooks
as low sun startles sudden wetness into glory;
risen rivers coil and ripple so the land becomes
electric with their snakey forms and cold tension.

Water surfaces are subtle broken mirrors
brimmed with darks of hidden drowning pools
newly sculpted by the weathers whim.
Rivers push into fields, patch green shoots
with torn reflective sky; gulls float on grass,
unwieldy branches come adrift
inside the waterspeed
to eel into the graves and gardens lying low.
A heron waits
uncertain of these fast track currents
that could catch his wings and quickly
fold him into flotsam.

Flood warnings are out again.
There will be more wild weather
and the land remembers other year's disasters
when the balance changed and water-energy came
slipping into everything, challenging the solidity
of oaks, of roots and rocks and human certainty.

OCTOBER BLESSING

The leaves are blessing me, the falling leaves
are blessing me and the road, the falling fiery leaves
are generous with their blessings and include
my old silver Saab, a Dalmatian, the tax inspector
hurriedly crossing his camomile lawn and a slow worm
coiled like a copper torc in her sun-bliss by the rockery.

I have only to stand still and October blesses me
with her dry lizardy kisses; my arms are touched,
my white lifted face is touched briefly, delicately
bless, bless, bless…months caress me with their fortunes,
a whole year of months. I reach out joyously to all
this goldleaf rain, these papery dollars of light, this luck.

This winter will bring blessing even under ice, under snow
and sorrow. In my own boulevard the tax inspector and I
will be blessed with lucks printing their sudden colours
on our roads and careful lawns, the hound's coming and going.
The sleeping slow worm will teach me how to hoard
the leaves warmth and let their light filter into my heart,
leaching out the old year's toxins so we will wake in the green
Spring, shrug off the dust of our last skin and begin again.

FIRE HARE

I saw a brown hare in the wheatfield
   long ears pointed to the sun
like two sweetcorns of fire   blazing out

      Late summer air has thinned:
frail as organza this sheen it plays
briefly, over us   Without these mirrors
how would we see   the touch of fire
goldenness   all that is numinous

here?   We may only have   one moment
like the gilded hare   and if all else is dross
       I am also this

Thoth, when you weigh my heart
know that I have only come lately to sun
and these things my heart carries lightly
as a heron feather, grey as rain.

SONG OF THE WHEAT

This is the time
when Wheat sings under the world's breath –

if you place your ear to the ground
         – *even in granite town, Silver Street*
         – *or ring-fence garden, in fields wild with foxes*
you'll hear the long sussuration of Wheat.

The music tells how The Lady dances over the earth,
the hem of Her glittering skirt of light
trailing over cornfields where heavy heads sway,
         murmur, listen with ears on fire.

Mother -- they sing: *Madron, Corn Mother, Ker* -

The song of Wheat is summer's dawn blackbird
who sharpens the stone of her song
on the pale morning's crystal. On moony nights
the young owls dip and purr, carrying the corn's
shadow voices in and out of the starry apples,
who nod wisely, and swell. The song of Wheat
         – *Mother, Madron, Corn Mother, Ker* –
is the print of The Lady's footsteps
flowers growing slow and round with sweetness.
The song is hands full of seeds and babies fruiting
fine as thistledown, fat as chestnuts.

And this is the time when Wheat sings praise
for the warm mouth of The Lady's kiss,
the pulse of Her heart in wrist and stem,
the gift of Her golden body of love.

GREAT MOTHER WITH ME

Great Mother, I am preparing myself to be fit for you
to enter. I am trying so hard to get it right,
setting the altar correctly, not fumbling my invocation.

But it is hard to open my heart so you may enter me,
the hinge of my heart is fear-frozen – *but you have sent
the Sun's new rising to warm me and that helps.*
The handle of my heart refuses to turn through time –
*but you have sent the soft wind to unwind it
and that helps.* The frame has clenched round the door
to keep it tight shut and familiar, I push and push
but cannot shift it *until you send a lioness
to stand at my shoulder and help.* But I have no key
No key! I wail, and cry inconsolably
*until you send the magical herb that opens all locks
and place it on my lips. that green kiss helps*
so my heart swings open easily, like a lotus
and I find space, stars in darkness, infinity.

Then I see how the flowers on the altar are your smile
and that my cat has your eyes. I see your presence
is in every candleflame, your grace in crystal and stone.
I know now, that you are under and over and in,
you are with me always; even in times when my heart closes
and I have no memory, no words, no rituals – your love
surrounds me, I hear your heartbeat inside my own.

NIGHT SCENTED JASMINE IN JULY

Lady of the Moon
the white jasmine outside my window
is making me drunk with its sweetness so
        I become
        fifteen parts a moth
and the blossom is a moon-candle
its flame drawing me deeper, deeper
into fire   so I become
flight, fluttering the entrancing black air
over my heavy wings   Fire-dancing

        so I become
        each green turning branch
        spearhead leaf
        white flower - a star
of four points shining.

      Five parts of me is a singer.
I sing the jasmine perfume out to you
Lady of the Moon
        listen, listen
to the scent of whitefire   in the dark
        on the breeze

lovesong: offering of pollen on my hands.

IF THE MOON WAS STOLEN

Sometimes Moon is wilful or angry with me and she slides out of view, goes absent, entering the round hole of her bat black cave where she stands blackly, furious, Crow–Moon fingers jabbing so hard at my Universe I can feel them twisting my muscles like black electric eels. This is Moon as witch-sister, dark-deeds Moon, perverse as stiletto.

Yet I know Moon has my interests deep at heart. I know her to be Motherly, balmlight over the sickness of fracturing dreams that crumple me up like yellowed paper, dreams of slow crackling ice, of aloneness. Moon, Moon lean down to me, place your lucent pearl face close to my white paper face, breathe light over me. Heal me, heal me.

Suppose someone entered the sky with intent and a fancy paraphernalia of lasers and fears? Suppose they raced up the steep titanium mesh of their own invisible staircase, crept up on the Moon (when she would be blissfully sleeping, laid on her side with one arm tucked under her cheek like the goddess at Hal Safleini) and they took her captive?

I've seen the scenarios of power working. All the wide streets of the sky would suddenly swarm with hoards of armoured marines and electric signalling, chain-link fencing flung in a trice over Taurus, Orion's power mined with a quick field of dragonsteeth. Patrols would be hair-trigger nervous, waiting for action – and she'd keep changing, spinning

through tender vulnerable slender into her wide fullness, closing her eyes into black. They'd apologise to everyone for their iron prison rooms and the absence of starlight but slowly explain they could no longer expose themselves or their people to the risks of her light and its terrible potentials of poetry and madness and howling and beauty.

But even if I could no longer see her, I'd still remember she was there. First there would be Grieving, ashy and tearful, then Starving and Eating. And I'd not be the only one. How can we measure the turning months? How can we dance the way the cat and the owl taught us? How can we dream?

We'd grieve, and weep rivers under the river. We would cry a new ocean and be part of its rising tide, going out in the dull blankness and danger of metal nights under their shield of tungsten and gunmetals, night after night, we would go and call like wolves for her, like green creatures primal in needs and bones, wanting the echoes of stars, the comforts of cloud-wings in the small hours.

And soon we'd invent a symbol, a bright mixture of sulphur and mithrael in equal parts, a silvery waxen shining like some soul-secret we'd always held in our hearts. Then the tide turning. Got any moonlight? people would whisper, craving, determined, slipping into a hidden crack in the grey town.

Around the world our pale candles beginning one to another at first, tiny sparks faint as mica on basalt. Secret illegal flames would burn at meeting points – those dry underground wells that we meant to restore several years ago – where we'd gather in twos and threes to tell the stories: Hare in the Moon, Moon Dew, Moon Lodge, The Drowned Moon, Macha Alla, Gala, Hina, Selene, Luna...

I know eventually there would be conflagration. That first sad quarter of grief would wax into Fury and we'd all become fire, our light streaming out like one great harvest moon challenging whatever, whoever, thought they could limit our skies or our poetry, our wildness, our lunacy, our wheeling, shapeshifting tempers of darkness and light.

And what would wane in us would be fear of blind night and the deepest black cave in ourselves. We would know them now, intimately; not as place of diminishment, cold as an iron vice without flicker of mood or beauty, but as space for beginning and learning; remembering that fire and stardust are always there at the source of ourselves.

Suppose the Moon was stolen, I think we could break any cage that held her, set her free by all the mirrored power of the Moon inside us. We'd connect, each to another, and together we'd chant the mad moon-poem named Love to reclaim her – blazing her silvers – bring her back home to our hearts and the dreaming dark of the world .

INSIDE THE MOON

Inside the Moon
Changing Woman plaits her hair
with silver thread. The black lake
of night is all her glass.

Patterns
        shiver through the senses of her hair
          and out   far beyond the stars

            I feel them here

they come in the form of early summer moths
shimmering on the window pane.
Like Changing Woman they are dressed in ivory
and are messengers of time, seasons: rhythms
        of the flowering of the first
      and the last   red rose.

MOTHER'S BONES

i.o.m.

my mother, Edith, my mother, Prudence

WARBABIES:1939-1945

Everything was breaking up: pieces of time
fragile as gilded Crown Derby
snapping in hurried fingers,
bloomed gold scoured off the skin and order
unravelling its scarlet chenille in the graveyards -
The tables and chairs stand exposed to the red-flecked wind,
trees hug themselves,
hold tight to their awful, unseasonable nakedness.
Tea is poured at exact clock chimes
when voices bigger than gods come piping
into the hearth and she makes her American lipstick
colour her in again, wiping plaster-dust meticulously
out of her mirror and her sharp white face.

She owns a neat shaped tin, rounded and orderly,
and she knows where her hands are, as she clasps it.
Her hands are not flying out from the ends of her arms
frantic birds seeking the children,
sifting fire, burning oil, broken stone for the children
blackened flesh raw blood bubbled skin smoking bone
of the children.

No, you clasp a good tin,
a bready tin marked with a safe slogan: *Hovis*.
A smiley tin from another time when the curtains
were spring-washed and children were lambs in green.
When bare lion-legs and grasping oak-talons
were subsumed in decent brown velvet.
Someone has just cut the future out of your shape –
SNIP, like that.   You remember your lessons: Three Fates,
Clotho, Lachesis, Atropos – *She who Cuts the Thread*.
She who is winding herself through hanging icicle glasses
who is sliding under the dangerous sherry-rims

and cut graphite pages, who advances from all four
shivering corners of the living room;
the snake-jaws of her scissors clicking, clicking.
You believed in some length of life once,
– blonde silk unrolling over the sky
in blaze and gentleness – but now you dare not.
You have fallen, you are falling continuously,
going down into blackness, the abyss.
Sometimes your hands graze touchstones:
the old horsehair sofa skirting you, bleeding
its powerful black wires electric over space,
the girl-lamp encircling, newly emptied of light.
Your hands cling, close on emptiness.
There's nothing to house you here, all the sharp stars
have burst through the ceiling, left hairline cracks
all over the sky. No Mothers are here,
nor Fathers, no one to spin the fine flax of your glory
over their spindle-fingers, no one to measure
the moon of your stretching skin.
No one here but you dancing,
a sycamore seed spinning down through the black,
pale tulle floating sweetly on air.
Hands appear out of space, brush past
with a rush of tinsel music, the fumbling chiming
of musical chairs, stroking and grasping.
Mouths open and close
speech drunk by the thirsty mumbling dark.
You drift, polished wood furniture arms and legs
revolving and gleaming slowly past you;
place-settings knifing reflections, candlelight
eaten away at the edge.
She is searching the roasted walls
for the place of love. She has seen a sign:
a neat-cuffed finger, pointing,
a sign to the place on the tin marked *Hovis*.
In her hands the round metal box beams

emerald Aladdin's lamp: green grass and trees;
held to her ear she hears the high flute of a bluebird,
the echoing clack of the weaver's loom so close
she can feel the warp and weft of perfect light.
This is her lodestar: scratched paint
on a tin of dreams.

The children are sown haphazard
over the lodestar fields.
She has flung them away into pictures
of heaven, places she's never been.
the children come out down her falling black chute.
Poised cells, their fingers-nets spread out to catch her
but she is falling past
into other levels of darkness,
the tin clutched safe in her hands,
prints of cornfields and rivers of clear shining water
streaming out of her eyes.

The babies spin slowly away,
unmoored engines and fragments, their hands milling air,
mouths open to blackness
rushing past sucking their sounds.
They spin out into different gravities
and she falls past
eyes shut, crayoned mouth in a small red ring of O,
feet neatly together in their very best Saturday shoes.
Her hands are folded one over the other over
her precious painted tin, one finger
hooked in the slack of sweet turquoise tulle.

Memories of falling shot into the genes, into the heart
of the starfish child spinning alone in the dark.
Babies wake in the fields, dragon's teeth,
so many warbabies sown into somewhere else.

They crawl over mud, listen to black sky popping
with terrors; they collide and touch, recoil
from the wrong shapes of these lumpy fraught creatures
whose tunes are pitched at the same cry of love.
Boys and girls at birth hauled out and packed up,
wrapped in brown paper, red wax bleeding over the knots
The children waking lost in a place
where their palms can't pattern the shape of familiar walls.
Their eyes learning how houses lurch to the arms
of trees burning the scarlet silk wind;
how wardrobes tilt limp blues of foxtrotting dresses
high in the vivid air, how the place of love floats
inaccessible: candlewick, lace, jug,
flower-glazed dishes standing precisely in space.
No bluebirds are singing here.

The child is searching for something to hold.
She turns over twigs and bones, startles
at carved lion's feet running away in foursomes,
tails of chenille unravelling behind.
The scissors are stalking and clacking
and she burrows into the shadows, finds
the dreaming warp and weft of perfect light
and places it safely under her tongue.

FIRST MAP

The Good Cupboard is always warm as comfort
humming slightly, the kind of droning sing-song
of someone completely happy in their work.

White lace pressed into ideal submission,
white starched sheets turned edge to middle
white traycloths embroidered with tiny stitches

where a woman in a flounced blue crinoline
is watering flowers from her green watering can;
the flowers are posies of knot stitch, palest pink

Under the Mary Mary garden
there is a contrary deer slip-stitching away
from the singsong heat that would smother her

mother her in tight white arms, kissing, singing,
hissing *this is the right way darling*
the white way tidy and clean, no stains.

But what was the map the stains made before
they were bleached beyond believing? What route
did the deer trace in the sweat of moonlight?

The whiteness has taken the form of a ghost
who squats and sews, takes up space in the corners,
biting the cotton in the black gash of her breathless mouth

as she patches and seams, killing time, turning
the ragged sheets back onto themselves, as if she sewed
shut the pages of books that must never be read.

BLOOD FATHER

Knowing his name would be to own something of him,
take something of his power, surely? So
over the years, slow drop by drop information appeared
in copperplate and text: a ship, a town, a time,
a man named for a gallows speechifier,
someone of silver-tongued passion
whose death-mask is as finely drawn as a woman's.

To set beside that there was my first-time landing off the ferry
pregnant and innocent and knowing everything
through the subtle senses of the blood; a recognition
that ached in the island-bones of stone, the bones
of my back, this architecture of descendants.
*This place and I have some meeting point that hangs
star-like, incarnadine, splintering light.*

Later, I tried to find his memory or even his uncoloured ghost
in the New Country where death took so many in despair.
I found only that names are thin and weak as tissue
and he was less than the place where one breath
had spoken his name into the hazy petrol air
that fumed like alcohol over the boardwalks of Main Street.

Only what was strange, was I saw so many deer
at the edges of shadowed woods and highways
that the people grew nervous of me
and turned their warmth into unwritten memos.

Under the swaying sibilant trees at the graveyard on the hill
I could get closer; the summer wind
had some greenness in it and the echo of something
evocative as lament. Or was it

that I was already making the story my son will carry?
My son and I are not strangers to the fabulous; we know how
to speak the language of animals and the prayers
that take us to the other country in dreams. These words
carry more inheritance than newspaper cuttings or boat-lists,
or a mossed grave-stone, cold and brilliant as a lost emerald.

MY BLUE DRESS

I dreamed I was making a dress, blue tulle and smocking
but my stitches were too loose and missed out lines
so the work was not tight and ridged but made
a new pattern of how to make the dress to fit the dance
white net and the click click click of kitten heels
my big skirt puffed on a wire round my knees
and I felt like a flower, a flower
and in my dream someone told me it wasn't right.

And I thought how hard it was for me to make a dress
like my Mother wore, a drifting blue dress pleated flat
over false breasts and red radiated skin. How she sewed!
All my childhood dresses, smocking and traycloths
and tapestry firescreens, everything flowed
out of her clever fingers, crimson chains and wreaths,
the hunt with twelve hounds and one deer racing for life
through the straight-stitch forest of viridian silks.
Her hands never idle, always the bright eye of the needle
watching out for the next place to stab and thread.

I was always inside the dream, clumsy fingered,
but I had to learn to be useful sensibly cross-stitching aprons,
hemming my cotton skirts. So I found deceit early,
hiding my books under yards of gingham
and hiding my dreamlife under the books
and I felt like a flower in the forest
where Wind's god-hands squeeze tight round
the throats of frail trees and shake shake
shake so hard that their green breath
rasps harsh as the sea drowning land

I think every stitch I ever made wanted Time
to burst every seam apart and I wanted (unknown, deep down

in my drifty mermaidy self) I wanted to whirl out from
the quiet windowseat and buy a blue bell-skirted dress
in Beatties, go dancing out of the Cancer House
with my small breasts flying like flags and my kitten heels
clicking syncopation over the slow rattle and roll of death.

SEA BED

I was small as a fish, sloppy-boned, slippy,
darting around in that back-and-forward aimless way
of little fish, no concentration in them,
no focus or refusal to see the wide bed
with its green-lit canopy of chiffons and weeds
burning phosphorescent in decay.
Nothing moved except white window lace
shivering in the slight winter wind.
Mother lay like sea-carved ivory. Open-mouthed
her skull's smile did not reach her eyes
which watched some other door begin to open
brightness creeping round the frame like dawn.

Such an ornate bed beneath the sea, so wide;
walnut scrolls and veiling, silver-green
grey brocade. I watched the water
gently moving shells and seaweeds
a little at a time, a little at a time
as if the tide had somehow lost its breath.
Nothing else alive here, no enfolding shoals.

I hung and darted, hung and darted
aimlessly in and out the doorway, but
became aware of black rock's weight above me,
of water's thick greenness, glassiness above me:
if I screamed, I'd be soundproofed out.

Someone held her mirror to her lips, looked in
as she had done, searching out an elusive
spark of life; cold blue enamelled eye it lay
beside the sharp silver-handled comb she used
to scrape and plait and pull and tame my wild hair.

When the mermaids claimed me, streamed out the glass
to take me deep, my inheritance of comb and mirror
cracked and fractured in my fierce hands.

HEAVY AIR

Some days I just stop and want you, my love,
 here beside me
– even though you'll be home in an hour or so
and nothing is wrong – it's a need to charm the Fates
as if I could wear the nearness of love as an amulet.
On these days, if you return unexpectedly
then even light releases its breath.

I don't breathe easy. I'm too aware
of the preciousness of air, its vitality
held in such a fragile vessel as a body.
Such a slight thing – a sigh – to hold a life.

I feel it now, high in the quick shallows,
air sucked in and out so fast I try to compensate,
breathe deeply until everything constricts and I
could drown. I don't remember my mother

    a wave of pale blue tulle, ruched and full, perfume
      – they were going dancing.
I must have been involved with those little pots of rouge,
white downy powderpuffs. She showed me
the absence of her breasts. Scorched maroon skin's texture
rough and mottled and a hollowness, as if her selfness
had been burned in to the bone.

Sea-whispers rustling between every snowy tissue layer
in the box that held the folded dress. My sudden breasts
terrifying as first blood.

Christmas: blue cedars heavy with snow, sunset
firing the smooth white shadowed garden: stillness.

When she died, the whirlpool of her breathing
collected every living breath within the house to sough
and rattle, rasp within her branded concave chest
the whole house breathless   and black
filtering under the doors like suffocating ash.

I can't remember her. There's too little, only this
constricting legacy of heavy air around the heart
and this need sometimes, for the simple anchor of your kiss.

MOTHER'S BONES

Under the green-glass fathoms Mother's bones
have come apart, sprawled loose across
her counterpane of grey brocade, lolled
into the swaying whispering caresses of the sea.

Her bed is disintegrating. As if someone
has cut all the stitching, all the careful
constructions of embroideries and tapestries,
all the smooth joins of her cages and frames
– it is all slowly drifting apart:
linen blooms under the cusp of anemones,
furbelows and corals twine walnut scrolls,
pale, hazy muslins flicker aquamarine.

My gaze is a torch delineating her long bones,
stroking the arch of her ribs, shining straight
into the empty sockets of her staring-back skull.
Her stark body was laid out in the dark
a childhood ago, now her skeleton has released
the force that kept her fixed and the sea
nuzzles gently *move on, move on move on* –
The patient sea is undoing each knot of memory
that I wound round her bones like tender kelp.

Frail with light, Mother's chosen bones
are floating skywards. As flute and drumstick,
as cup and oracle they leave the sea bed
to its own transformation and begin to sing.

INDEX OF FIRST LINES

ACKNOWLEDGEMENTS

Some of the poems reproduced here have appeared in the magazines *Acumen, Fire, Scintilla, Envoi, Quattrocentro, Lapidus Magazine, New Welsh Review,* and the anthologies *The Book of Hopes and Dreams* (bluechrome), *Images of Women* (Arrowhead), *The Allotment* (Stride), *Into the Further Reaches* (PS Avalon) *Poetry Pool* (Headland) and the *We'Moon Diary.*

Other poems have been prize-winners in: *The Petra Kenny International Poetry Competition, the Cardiff International Poetry Competition, Second Light, Nottingham, Salisbury House,* and others.

 PS AVALON PUBLISHING

About PS Avalon

PS Avalon Publishing is an independent and committed publisher offering a complete publishing service. As a small publisher able to take advantage of the latest technological advances, PS Avalon Publishing can offer an alternative route for aspiring authors in our particular fields of interest.

As well as publishing, we offer an education programme including courses, seminars, group retreats, and other opportunities for personal and spiritual growth. Whilst the nature of our work means we engage with people from all around the world, we are based in Glastonbury which is in the West Country of England.

new poetry books

Our purpose is to bring you the best new poetry with a psychospiritual content, work that is contemplative and inspirational, with a dark, challenging edge.

self development books

We publish inspiring reading material aimed at enhancing your personal and spiritual development in which everything is kept as simple and as accessible as possible.

PS AVALON PUBLISHING

Box 1865, Glastonbury,

Somerset BA6 8YR, U.K.

www.psavalon.com

info@psavalon.com

Lightning Source UK Ltd.
Milton Keynes UK
20 October 2009

145201UK00001B/5/P